# KING CARP WATERS

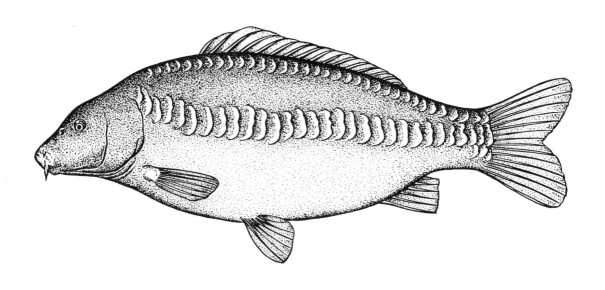

# THE KING CARP WATERS

## Chris Ball

The Crowood Press

First published in 1993 by
The Crowood Press Ltd
Ramsbury, Marlborough
Wiltshire SN8 2HR

**British Library Cataloguing in Publication Data**

A catalogue record for this book is available from the British Library.

ISBN 1 85223 726 0

**Acknowledgements**
The picture appearing on page 11 is reproduced with the kind permission of the Marchant Lane Collection.

Line drawings by Brian Atkins.

**Dedication**

In general, many people over the years have helped in my quest for information on all matters related to that magical fish, the carp. But I'm an incurable anyway – the whole extravaganza that goes with carp fishing is something I thrive on. So, to my many friends I extend my thanks.

In the preparation of this book special mention must go to several people: first, to Brian Atkins, an artist and fisherman whose outstanding drawings were produced from my very 'rough' images jotted down on a piece of paper; and to another man who gave 'up and beyond the call of duty'– Mike Wilson – without whose help the Savay chapter would have been somewhat empty!

Finally, I also applaud the constant encouragement that my wife Lynne and the rest of the family have given me. Night after night they would see me bent over the keyboard with an occasional glass of port in my hand, writing down the story of a very special fish – the king carp!

Chris Ball
Frimley
Surrey

Typeset and designed by:
D & N Publishing
DTP & Editorial Services
The Old Surgery
Lambourn
Berkshire RG16 7NR

Phototypeset by FIDO Imagesetting, Witney, Oxon

Printed and bound in Great Britain by
BPCC Hazell Books Ltd
Member of BPCC Ltd

Throughout this book the pronouns 'he', 'his' and 'him' have been used to refer to both men and women.

# CONTENTS

## FOREWORD

Donald Leney did as much as Dick Walker to open angler's eyes to the potential of carp fishing. Don't forget that forty years ago a carp angler was as rare as a burbot, and if it wasn't for Leney names like Redmire, Billing and Savay would never have entered our vocabulary, the angling world would never have been jaw-dropped by the astonishing news of Walker's 'forty-four' and I would never have caught my 'fifty-one'.

Unlike Walker, however, it was never Leney's intention to widen the appeal of carp. He was primarily a trout farmer, but one who had more than just a passing interest in other species – notably carp and catfish. He supplied trout to fisheries up and down the UK, but though he also supplied carp these were not in those days destined for angling waters. Most of the carp went to private estate lakes where they were intended as either a kind of natural ornamentation or, as in the case of Redmire, a method of natural weed clearance. In stocking these waters Donald Leney unwittingly made angling history.

Leney did not just have a professional interest in carp; he liked them for themselves. 'They have fascinating characteristics,' and he devoted a lifetime's study to them. It is to every carp angler's regret that he never published or even kept the results of his observations. He was perhaps too modest and unassuming to think that others might profit from his studies, but he certainly had the qualifications for such work, having read Biology at Oxford and having made fish culture his profession. To me, however, Leney was not just the person who seeded Redmire with monsters and so altered our angling lives, he was one of my greatest friends.

I first met him in 1980 after he had written to congratulate me on catching my fifty-one-pounder, and for the next six years I visited him regularly. He lived in a beautiful, rambling nineteenth-century home near Haslemere and I have many happy memories of epic tea-times there.

*Donald Leney releases young carp into a Surrey water over thirty years ago.*

6

His housekeeper, Mrs Packham, would have baked a special 'slab' cake, and after toast and home-made raspberry jam this cake was cut. Then, over the second pot of tea, the carp talk would begin – and it would continue unabated and enthusiastically into the evening and then into the night. Sometimes our conversation would veer towards other subjects, like flowers and reptiles, on which matters he was also an authority. Sometimes we might consider other species of fish, but always we came back to our main theme: the carp.

However, it wasn't because he was so keen on my favourite fish that he became such a friend. I liked him because of his generous spirit, his sense of humour and the fact that he had such an intense interest in all life. He was in his eighties when I knew him and, though partly crippled by arthritis, he was always optimistic, sharp-minded, curious and enthusiastic. In all, he was a wonderful character, but fond memories are carrying me away.

Donald Leney was an extremely pleasant and very distinguished gentleman who, almost by accident, created one of the greatest carp waters in the United Kingdom. I am sure he would have been both flattered and honoured by this timely record of some of his most famous achievements.

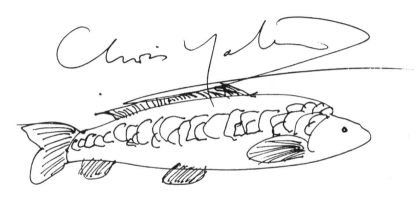

## PREFACE

This book has been a while in coming to fruition, for if the truth be known, I had a more than even chance nearly twenty-five years ago of publishing a work on Redmire Pool's early days. It was at a time when I first became friendly with Dick Walker, having originally contacted Dick along with other members of the Carp Catchers' Club to ask them for a picture of their historic Redmire twenty-pounder (though not all had caught a beast of such size). The response was tremendous, and after much detective work I managed – even though the trail seemed vague at times – to collect pictures of all those big carp. Dick Walker later suggested to me that these photographs along with their respective capture stories could be bundled together to form a book of great interest to anglers generally, and carp anglers in particular. At that time Dick had all the contacts open to him in the publishing field... however, I never pursued it, though the pictures did not go to waste, for years later they formed part of the early section of that marvellous book published in 1984 – *Redmire Pool* by Kevin Clifford and Len Arbery (Beekay Publishers).

It was perhaps that volume which sparked off the idea for this book. Besides wanting to broaden the scope of Redmire considerably I had thoughts of other outstanding carp waters, for the development and catches during their formative years are just as absorbing. However it would have taken a book the size of a house to cover in depth all the big carp waters I know of, so within the pages that follow you will find six of the best. Some are famous, but by contrast, others you might not be so familiar with.

When one looks at these remarkable waters, a common denominator soon becomes apparent: they were all stocked with a fast-growing European domestic strain of fish – the 'king carp'. Of these the most beautiful, impressive and fastest growing were the 'Galician' strain. They originally came from careful selective breeding and were, in essence, a jumble of many eastern European breeds. These carp became available in the UK as long ago as 1870, though the general

NOTES ON COARSE FISH.

A FINE KING CARP.

The King Carp.—This is a quick-growing variety of the Common Carp, also known as the Mirror Carp, its skin is for the most part bare of scales, where it is not bare scales are of large size and iridescent giving

*A page from an early* Surrey Trout Farm and United Fisheries *catalogue.*

public became far more aware of king carp through a small fish farm near Haslemere in deepest Hampshire. This business was called the Surrey Trout Farm and United Fisheries. One man's name is synonymous with the Surrey Trout Farm and its carp – Donald Leney. For it was he, perhaps more than anyone else, who changed the face of carp fishing in the UK and can truly be regarded as the modern father of the movement. In today's technology-driven world of carp fishing, few people realize how or even why carp were introduced to our waters!

So, this book is an anthem to a handful (the cream) of these lakes (and one river) that Donald Leney stocked with the much-loved 'Leney' carp. The extensive research and all-important photographic material needed for a book such as this – I have collected data since the early 1960s – have resided largely in my fishing den, the Carproom,

'The mighty Galicians . . .'

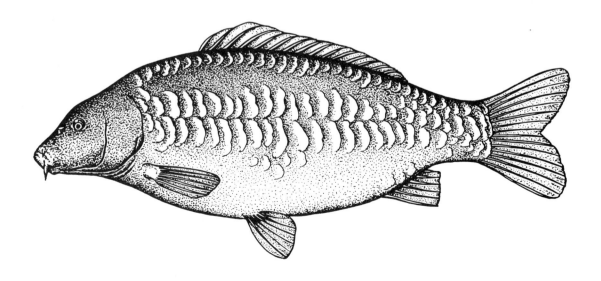

*Another stocking takes place...*

until now. However, you might have read at some time in the past articles written by me on the topic of 'Leney' carp. Throughout the chapters that follow I have tried to include as many of these photographs as possible, but where no picture was available to illustrate a point in time I commissioned a drawing of the scene. Anyway, enough of the technical side of the book...the Leney carp are far more important than any of this.

So, raise if you will a toast with me to Donald Leney, the Surrey Trout Farm and the mighty 'Galicians' – the equivalent of which we are unlikely ever to see again...

Chris Ball
Frimley Surrey

# 1 OF CARP...

In the early part of this century many of the carp that swam in British waters were of the so-called 'wild' strain. These are the long, thin common carp to which we loosely refer these days as 'wildies'. For years before this century they were one of the backbones of the Christian monks' diet, for these carp dwelt in specially created 'stew ponds' and were successfully caught once a week – on a Friday – for the dinner table. The brassy-scaled mirror carp and its derivatives were a rarity, with few lakes or rivers holding them.

The simple reason for this scarcity was that imports into England of any coarse fish were nothing like the scale that we saw, for instance, in the 1960s. However, I have recently seen at auction in London five mirror carp in a glass case, the date indicating that they were captured in 1905. If this is correct then they amounted to an unusual catch at the time – possibly the reason why the captor had killed them, for none weighed more than 5lb. So, how did the mirror carp and its brethren become indigenous to this country? To answer this we have to look no further than one man and his 'soft spot' for carp – Donald Leney.

Educated at New College, Oxford as a fresh-water biologist, Leney started in the fishery business with his father Douglas in the 1920s. Seventy years ago there was little interest in carp as a sporting species in the UK and gladly no appetite for eating them either! However, just as this book is going to press, noted historian Kevin Clifford has released valuable information which shows that a company in England did indeed deal with considerable numbers of king carp during the latter part of the last century. This business was called the Manor Fisheries and was based in Lincolnshire. The proprietor was Thomas Ford who dealt in carp by buying them from Holland.

In 1907 Thomas Ford's Manor company was purchased by a conglomerate which was later renamed The Surrey Trout Farm and United Fisheries Ltd. This was the initial trigger for carp with the young Donald Leney. Though it must be remembered first and foremost that he and his father were breeders and suppliers of trout, Donald fortunately considered that carp were far more interesting, and through Thomas Ford's

*A carp from the last century. (Reproduced with the kind permission of the Marchant Lane Collection).*

connections he started importing carp from Holland. There was more to this venture than meets the eye, for Donald would personally make the trip each autumn to the fish farm at Vaassen in northern Holland virtually to hand-pick the best grown of the stock. By his careful selection of these carp – one of the hardiest and most beautiful variety, the 'Galician' strain – Donald brought back carp that in the years to come would provide the foundation of modern carp fishing. They were special in many ways:

1. An attribute displayed was an extraordinarily long growing cycle, the carp often not finishing their growth span until their fifteenth or sixteenth year.
2. They would grow quickly, often reaching 20lb in weight in less than seven years.
3. The coloration and scaling of the mirrors were spectacular, some displaying perfect linear scaling (one single row of mirror scale of equal size running along the entire lateral line). A few, perhaps the most dazzling carp we have ever seen in the UK, were of the fully-scaled mirror type.
4. Finally, they grew to a large size – in some cases enormously so.

Let me explain this long-term growing attribute in more depth. Carp – or any fish for that matter – only grow in bone structure and frame for a pre-determined period, and after this, the actual weight of the fish depends on many factors such as health, age, the amount of food available and so on. You might be surprised to learn that the Belgian, Italian and German carp strains introduced in such large quantities into UK waters during the late 1960s and early 1970s would be hard pushed to grow in bone structure beyond their tenth year. This doesn't mean that this kind of carp cannot grow into a very big fish, but they often have short, squat bodies with high backs and exceptionally deep flanks, coupled with sparse scaling and small fins. Look at pictures of carp that live in famous waters such as Leisure Sport's Match Lake at Yateley, or Homersfield in Norfolk and you will find that they characterize these creatures perfectly.

The fast-growing aspect of the 'Leney' carp came from selective breeding that had taken place on the Continent over many years. They had been bred, as many breeds were, for the table. For instance, in Germany to this day carp is the national Christmas dish (perish the thought!), as having less scales the mirror carp made the housewife's job easier when preparing the dish.

At once Donald Leney realized the sporting potential, handsome sleek looks and beautiful

*Donald Leney in his study at Haslemere in Surrey.*

*'Some displayed perfect linear scaling.' Redmire, 1956.*

scaling of these 'Galician' carp. He knew that by picking the fastest growers of each year batch he would have fish that could grow quickly in a short space of time and offer the angler an adversary that would fight both long and hard – how true. He transported the fish over in huge cans protected by wicker baskets, and they were held in ponds at either Haslemere in Surrey (the main depot) or at Nailsworth in Gloucestershire – a further subsidiary of the trout farm.

This then was the situation around 1925 when The Surrey Trout Farm started supplying carp to the general public. The term king carp was an umbrella name then, for it covered all the known varieties of the commercially bred carp, including mirror, leather and common carp. You often saw reported in the press during the 1950s that

so and so had captured a 'king' common carp, or that the captor had landed a 'king carp'.

The Surrey Trout Farm was almost the only outlet for king carp in the UK at this time. Business was slow to start but this did not bother Donald, for he dealt in almost all kinds of freshwater fish besides trout. Indeed, he supplied fish to all the major aquariums and institutions as well as to individuals, angling clubs and associations. His 'soft spot' for carp culminated in the farm advertising the fact that here was a fast-growing, strong-fighting freshwater fish that grew quickly . . . he started to receive enquiries! Perhaps the most significant order received was on 10 March 1934, for this consignment of fifty kings was delivered to an estate lake deep in Herefordshire – Redmire!

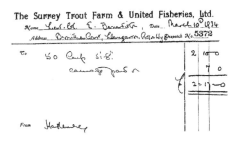

*This advertisement for the* Surrey Trout Farm *appeared in the angling press in January 1952. Many angling clubs and associations did 'try some'!*

*'Perhaps the most significant order received.' The historic Redmire invoice.*

*Just one of the Leney record books. They were passed on after Donald's death to Chris Yates. This particular volume covers the years 1950–3.*

The following year, Little Billing in Northampton was to receive a batch of these magical carp. In these waters the carp grew well, with both producing fish in excess of 40lb and with larger fish being seen especially at Redmire. Looking through Leney's records you can see how the growth of his carp business started to gain pace as the acceptance of carp for stocking purposes became more popular. However, it would be twenty years before the real rush started as people like Dick Walker advocated that anglers, clubs and associations should stock with carp.

One major point that has come to light in recent years about fish growth, is that places like Redmire and Billing received little or no fishing pressure during the carp's all-important growing period – the first twenty years. The larder was full to brimming when the fish were stocked and with little or no competition from other fish nature took its course – somewhat spectacularly. When anglers arrived on the scene to fish these waters, both held huge fish and ones that were far larger than those eventually caught. I include Chris Yates' record 51lb 8oz mirror in this scenario! The escalating events surrounding specialist fishing in the early 1950s revolved mainly around carp as people became aware that they were at

last catchable – and anglers then urged clubs to stock with king carp.

The list of carp stockings is almost endless when we look at Leney's record books. They are all in there: Savay, Ashley Pool, Hemmingford Grey (Eggets), Bracken Lake, Stoneham Lake, Frensham Small Pond, Dartford, and many of the gravel pits in the Colne Valley as well as estate lakes in and around the Surrey area. Northern carp anglers need not worry, for thousands were shipped to the Midlands and further north, but what happened to them, God only knows. There is some scope here for you northern carp anglers – all you have to do is find the waters . . . perhaps easier said than done! Although we know where stockings took place, or should I say we have found most of the lakes by now, believe me that there are still some lakes where these carp have been left unmolested for years!

A nice footnote to this is that Chris Yates and Bob James have found somewhere in their locality (the Avon Valley) an original Leney water that was stocked as per Leney's records on 2 January 1933 with 200 kings. Who knows what they'll turn up?

I have been lucky enough to catch a few of these highly prized Leney fish myself, so I talk from some experience – they really are something else, the very big ones often found approaching 3ft in length and totally immaculate. Imagine, my first English 30lb carp was an unknown fish from an unknown water, and was a magical Leney mirror...

So far I have said little about fully-scaled mirrors, for here we find some the finest examples of the 'Leney' strain. There seems to be two sorts:

1. The large-scaled type. These have enormous mirror scales which completely cover the body. I've been fortunate just once to have seen one which lived in Frensham and was caught only the odd time. When disaster struck this carp very nearly survived. I visited the place where it was in 'hospital' at the NRA fishery depot in Guildford. Every morning and evening for five days I visited this grand fish, praying it would survive. Often I

had the chance to observe it at very close range, and it remains one of the most impressive carp I've ever seen. Its dimensions were 33 × 25in and it weighed 28lb 2oz. With great sadness I have to tell you that it did not survive, but died on 21 February 1987.

Another beautiful 'Leney' fully-scaled mirror was one of the fish that Bob Reynolds caught at Billing in the late 1950s, this one weighing 27lb 9oz.

2. Small, even-scaled type. These can look like a common carp at a quick glance, but the scales are more brassy. The best example I can think of is Jack Opie's 27lb 5oz fish which was caught in September 1954 from Redmire Pool.

Moving on to the linears, Redmire was full of them; Chris Yates' record is one, Frensham had a few, and so did the Electricity Cut and the

*A young Kevin Clifford holds a 'large-scaled type' – a fully-scaled mirror from Redmire.*

*'Small, even-scaled type' – a fully-scaled mirror, and at the time Britain's largest. Jack Opie's 27lb 5oz Redmire beauty.*

*One of Frensham's linear specials.*

Army Lake in Hampshire. The ones I've seen looked like carved pieces of wood, being mostly dark bronze, reddish or yellow in colour – in other words, breathtaking! I myself have recently landed one of over 30lb. It had proportions the like of which you just don't see anymore – just over 36in to the tip of the tail and a 26in girth... Fantastic!

I guess one of the lasting enigmas that carp fishing has to offer is the Redmire 'monsters'. These fish were seen at Redmire by responsible anglers over a period of some thirty years. Forget forty-pounders and bigger – these carp would stretch the realms of our imagination beyond belief. Jack Hilton no less, once reported seeing a 4ft-long common on the Redmire shallows, and it had a proportional width and depth to go with it! Years before that, Master Carpcatcher Maurice Ingham watched for a whole afternoon a monster that was 'at least 3ft 6in long' and 1ft across the back! I have Mike Wilson to thank for finding, in recent years, the Carp Catchers' Club rotary letters, in which there is much discussion on the monsters. Chris Yates has tales that make you shake with excitement, then sheer terror enters your mind as you realize that he really did see these extraordinary carp – when he told me about

*The late Tom Mintram with a gorgeous Redmire Pool common carp of well over 20lb. 'All-scalers' were comparatively rare within the Leney stockings.*

*Near 3ft-long Leney from Frensham. This sparsely scaled 30lb mirror fell to the author in the summer of 1983.*

them I had to reach for a drink in double-quick time!

A final comment on this monster theme. After Jack Hilton had seen that unbelievable 4ft monster on the shallows, the story got back to Dick Walker. Dick, as only Dick could, worked out that a fish like this with Redmire proportions might weigh anywhere from 90lb to 120lb. The trouble was that Hilton was quite happy to accept that figure saying 'I saw what I saw' and adding,

'if that fish is ever landed, you could throw away the record books...forever!'

Donald Leney was both surprised and heartened when he heard the stories of monster Redmire carp and others...he never expected 'his' carp to go on to become the creatures of myth.

Donald Leney died in October 1987 on the eve of the great hurricane – perhaps like the big wind he stirred our waters into life by introducing to them the resplendent 'Leney' king carp.

# 2 REDMIRE POOL – LENEY'S FINEST HOUR

*To trace Redmire Pool from its embryonic beginnings we will be drawn inextricably into the first stirrings of the modern carp fisher.*

## THE BEGINNINGS

By the simple expediency of constructing a dam across a small valley early in the 17th century, men with straining backs and sweat-covered brows transformed a small fold in the Herefordshire countryside into the most famous carp water this country has ever known – Redmire Pool. The estate this small reach of water lies within was named Bernithan Court, then in the ownership of one William Hoskyns who had instructed work to start on irrigation and general waterworks, hence the pool's origin. Whether this medium-sized lake contained coarse fish shortly after this time is hard to ascertain, but as

Mother Nature has proved countless times, she can secretly wave her magic wand…the first signs of fish life to swim in Bernithan Court's fertile water were probably the humble roach or tiny gudgeon.

This situation lasted some centuries, time in which we have no real knowledge of the pool and its contents, but come the early 1930s the property came into the possession of Lt.-Col. E. Barnardiston. As he was a man of considerable substance with strong country ties, he was naturally a keen sportsman and one of the first acts he performed on his new property was to stock the pool. This gives us the valuable link with Donald Leney, for delivered from the Nailsworth,

*Looking down the hill, one of the first pictures Dick Walker took of the pool.*

Gloucestershire branch of the Surrey Trout Farm came a quantity of prime trout. Casting a fly from the flat open area of the dam afforded the chance to catch a trout, but unfortunately no one is alive today to say whether this actually happened or not. What we do know, however, is that the trout did not thrive and gradually disappeared, although there is evidence to suggest that the odd cannibal trout lasted for many years. It is important to know that trout existed within the pool, because I have no doubt that it was their presence that led to the stock of gudgeon that thrived and also to the two chub which were seen there in the early 1950s. I'm sure the gudgeon and chub were brought as small livebaits by people who had permission from Mrs Barnardiston to fish for the trout. A most valuable informant who had knowledge of the pool and of the surrounding area was Jack (the Roadman) Farmer. I personally met this gentleman just once when years ago Chris Yates and I shared a pint of fine ale in the Royal Arms, this public house being but a short distance from the estate. This extraordinarily quiet, inherently country person had known Chris from the time he and Rod Hutchinson came to the pub in the early 1970s, this being a welcome break for the two young pretenders who were hell-bent on capturing a Redmire carp. Though in his time Jack had snatched many an eel from the pool, he no doubt had found a trout on the end of his hand-line too!

During the immediate years after the trout were released, events took a turn for the worse at the pool, the lake being full of all kinds of dense weed and algae which constantly caused problems by blocking the water supply intake to the big house. This fine property stands on the hill overlooking the valley and looks little different today. Who gave Lt.-Col. Barnardiston the idea to stock with carp, thereby giving the fish a chance to help clear the weed problem, is unclear, but it's my bet he had conversations with the Surrey Trout Farm. It was this farm – through Donald Leney – that suggested he stocked with young king carp.

It was a bold move for carp were still a rarity in England – indeed, as we have seen, they were also a comparative newcomer to the Surrey Trout Farm. But the order was firmed up once the decision was taken to purchase a consignment of fifty fish. The hand-picked carp had been imported personally by Donald Leney during the winter months and the delivery was scheduled for 10 March 1934. This batch of carp – confirmed by Donald himself – were two-year-old fish, for the delivery note shows them to be 5½ in to 8in in length. So, once the bill of £2-17-0d (£2.68) was paid, delivery took place.

The small carp were released into a haven of pure water, and with a larder full to brimming it's hard to think of anywhere better for a small head of carp to mature. Indeed, it was a paradise. Just as important, it was a paradise that held hardly any threats, least of all from anglers, for there's no evidence to suggest that anyone save the odd poacher ever visited the pool. Excepting the fact that a few fish perished through nature's fish hunters – herons, otters and maybe a cannibal trout – most of the little fish made it through to adulthood. By the end of World War II (in which time, thankfully, no bombs of war came near) many of the carp were big, and some were enormous...

**The First Anglers**

Naturally, anglers were about after the war and there can be little doubt that permission was granted to some who cared to ask Mrs Barnardiston, who was still in residence at the big house, her husband having passed away some years before. One such angler was John Munro, a local fisherman who has the distinction of being the first man to catch a Bernithan carp in the year of 1950. This specimen weighed 6lb, showing that the mature carp had successfully spawned, probably more than once. However, during the year before a chap named Harold Bolton had fished all one night and the next day quite by chance, owing to the River Garron being in flood. He was unsuccessful in catching anything, but fishing from a punt – a craft that is still in service as I write – at the shallow end, he saw monster carp cruising about near the surface. He, and possibly John Munro, were members of the Gloucester

*Bob Richards at the pool in 1951 – taken within days of the record-breaking capture.*

Anglers' Association and it was through this organization that a certain gentleman named Bob Richards (who had joined the club a little earlier) came into contact in the autumn of 1950 with Harold Bolton. He told Bob of this very private water at Llangarron.

Bob Richards, a Gloucestershire man and manager of a local tobacconist's shop, was a passionate fisherman and one who had fished for most species but who had become interested in carp through the writings of Denys Watkins-Pitchford ('B. B.'). In particular, Bob enjoyed the *Fisherman's Bedside Book* (Eyre and Spottiswoode Ltd), published in 1945. This book was

B. B.'s anthem to the fisherman and contained many stories on carp and their capture.

Like most aspiring carp fisherman of the period, the problem Bob faced was of finding somewhere to fish for carp. Joining the Gloucester Anglers' Association put him in touch with other anglers, although most fished in inter-club matches. However, Harold Bolton explained to Bob that he could doubtless get permission to fish Bernithan if he cared to try it. He explained the water was very weedy and difficult to fish from the bank. Bob, realizing that here was an excellent chance to fish locally for carp, wasted no time and fixed up for a visit by phone that very evening. He had permission to fish the following Thursday, and the owner requested that Bob call at the court for the paddle which enabled the old punt to be used – something Bob did on all occasions he visited the pool. The first and last visit to the pool for the season of 1950 was a blank day for Bob as regards catching carp, but he did see a big carp jump during the early evening and all the time had the feeling that here was a water that seemed special – in fact, very special, indeed.

He whiled away the winter and waited with growing anticipation for the following season to come round – how that time must have dragged by, but all the while with a burning passion glowing within his soul he knew he could wait. Like all fishermen the anticipation of what lay beneath the calm dark surface, let alone the exciting watery depths of Bernithan probably kept Bob awake some nights during this time.

As the 1951 season approached, Bob, with sky-high aspirations, contacted Mrs Barnardiston who informed him that he could fish there any time if he first rang up and let her know the day he wanted to go. Throughout this season Bob made some ten visits, often going with his friend John Thorpe. Before his record-breaking day only once before did he or his companion have a bite of any description. This carp shot off at a tremendously high speed for the centre of the lake, then bore down into weeds and got well and truly stuck, eventually slipping the hook. The weather that day had all the signs of the carp-catching conditions as told in B. B.'s *The*

*Fisherman's Bedside Book* – heavy storm clouds and thunder an hour after he had hooked that fish.

The carp had taken a baited hook of bread paste dipped in a pot of English honey, and the loss of this fish, the first after weeks of trying, made Bob more determined than ever. However, his next visit a fortnight later was also a blank day, but with some holiday coming up the following week he hatched a master plan. This included the son of one of the farm workers, who was not just any boy but one that would have a long-standing relationship with Redmire, his name being Eric Higgs. It would be young Eric who would bait up a couple of spots in the pool for Bob, putting in just a handful or so of marble-sized bread-paste baits every morning until Wednesday, 3 October. Bob had decided that that day would be the last visit of the season. The idea of baiting up had not come about by chance, for Bob had read of the groundbaiting method for carp and was keen to try it. Because his prior visits were usually made at the last moment, he could hardly hatch any plans for groundbaiting to take place, but on this occasion and with the benefit of these few days of holiday he put the plan into action.

Without the luxury of a car, Bob travelled from Gloucester to the estate by bus, arriving there at 11 a.m. Young Eric met him and together they walked down to the pool. He showed Bob exactly where he had baited up – an area roughly 20ft from the bank. While making his bread paste, Bob found that the temperature of the water felt warm to his hand, indeed the weather as such had been most clement of late and it was a proper Indian summer. The tackle used is worth looking at: an Allcock's Lancer rod (a mixture of whole cane and lancewood, and in essence a roach rod) an Ambidex casting reel and his line was Platil 6.1lb breaking strain. The hook was popular eyed type, size 10. The small cork float was set for a depth of 4½ft and the bait was as before – bread paste dipped in honey. Nobody else had been near the pool since his last visit and it could be said with some certainty that Bob was the one who fished the water consistently during 1951.

## Record Carp!

The spot to which Bob decided to cast his line – and where he had instructed young Higgs to bait – was beside the glorious weeping willow near the dam end on the western shore (later to become the Willow pitch), where there was a nice grassy bank area on which to settle his creel. He cast out after first dipping the bait into the honey pot, and settled back on his basket for a long wait. But within ten or fifteen minutes his float stirred to the first run of the day. Within a few minutes the fish was thumping its tail on the bank. It weighed exactly 5lb and was his first carp from the pool.

Rebaiting his hook, he had another run within ten minutes of casting, and on landing this fish he found it to weigh 4lb 5oz. These might seem very small to you and I, but remember that they were some of the first carp Bob had ever seen or landed.

At around 12.30 p.m. Eric left to go for his lunch and Bob too started on his, but a carp disturbed the proceedings as his float slipped away without fuss. This carp was perhaps four or five times the size of the previous fish, for it tore away quickly into deep water. Bob's previous luck then ran out as the line caught twice around the pick-up arm (half-bail) and jammed solid; needless to say it broke. He reeled in feeling shaken by the power of the run of this fish, something he had never before experienced but had often read about. He noticed that his hands were trembling as he tried to tie on a fresh hook.

Shortly afterwards, Eric came back and heard Bob's sad tale. Then as they sat there Bob received his fourth bite, this carp also shooting off at high speed, first one way and then the other. As the fish came close to the bank he felt a bump on the line and it was off! He estimated it at about 9lb. Casting out again, yet another bite was forthcoming. This fish became stuck and not even young Higgs with an armful of stones could shift it. Bob tried hand-lining but all to no avail, and eventually he wound in to find shot, hook and fish missing. Young Eric had never known excitement such as this, for most fisherman he'd seen at the pool usually left biteless and were never seen again.

After all this disturbance Bob decided to move round to the far side of the pool, just above the old boat house. By then it was 2.30 p.m. After half an hour without a sign of a carp and having calmed down somewhat he began to think he was foolish moving away from his baited area. So, at 3.15 p.m. he went back, put on a fresh bait, cast in and settled back, quite expecting a long wait for another bite. Lighting his pipe, he sat unknowing as a leviathan drew ever closer to his bait. Soon after, he experienced his sixth run of the day. This carp like the last went off at a rate of knots straight up the centre of the pool, but

this time it turned and came back towards Bob. Although feeling that this was a strong fish, Bob was able to control it better and the crazy, powerful runs always ended in him being able to turn the unseen monster. Lady Luck was again playing on his side, and once during the fight when the fish surfaced close to the bank young Eric, with eyes popping out of his head, changed the net for the gaff, Bob's net being far too small for a fish this size!

In all, the fight lasted some fifteen minutes before the big fish came to the bank. A botch-up with the gaff meant it ripped out, but a second

*Bob Richards and the young Eric Higgs – there lay a record carp!*

attempt held and with a strong heave Bob had it on the bank. He never again used a gaff on any carp he caught subsequently. What a sight confronted Eric and Bob as they viewed this enormous carp! Bob tried to weigh the beast but couldn't hold the scales steady enough, so he took it up to the court where it was weighed on accurate scales. He could hardly believe his eyes as the scale arm dipped slowly to 31lb 4oz...

It was owing to Mrs Barnardiston's kind offer to take Bob into Ross-on-Wye with his catch that he packed up at 6 p.m., otherwise he would have waited until the bus left Llangarron at 7 p.m. Can you begin to imagine what the uproar was like when he then boarded the omnibus from Ross-on-Wye to Gloucester?

The secretary of the Gloucester Anglers' Association, Mr T. M. Ellis, was contacted and the weight and authenticity was established beyond doubt. It was the next day that Bob Richards wrote to B. B. telling him of his great fortune. B. B. then contacted a certain Mr Richard Walker, and this was how Walker came to receive the fish to set it up. Meanwhile, Bob was as keen as ever and returned to Redmire for a further try on the Saturday (6 October). He hooked a carp at about 11.45 a.m., but as luck would have it he lost it when the hook broke!

On the Saturday Mrs Barnardiston invited a photographic friend over, her name being Miss Wight and she told her to 'Come over and take some photographs,' adding 'The man who caught the big (record) fish is coming again today.' Luckily, Miss Wight was able to get there and her pictures are the earliest known of Redmire, besides recording Bob on film at the pool as well. After both ladies departed, Bob landed yet another Bernithan carp, this time a common carp weighing in at 9lb. This proved to be the last fish of the season, but far from the last of what the angling world was to hear of Bernithan!

The tremendous uproar that the capture of Bob Richard's record carp caused in the popular press of the day was not surprising. Only a short time before the catch a noted ichthyologist had stated that carp in the wild were unlikely to exceed 25lb in weight, but now here was a fish

*Close-up of the 31lb 4oz record carp – a perfect example of a Leney linear.*

considerably over that size. The correspondence columns were full of it. Was it healthy, or was the extreme weight of the carp due to some abnormality or disease? All this speculation was silenced in a single convincing blow when Dick Walker wrote to the *Fishing Gazette,* stating that the flesh was all healthy and there was no reason why this carp should not be a new British record carp.

How the carp came to Dick Walker is a tale within itself. To start with, once Bob had shown the fish to family and friends he laid its corpse out on the coal heap in his back garden. Bob wasted no time in contacting B. B. who then put Dick Walker in touch with him, suggesting that he'd be pleased to mount the carp for him. Bob sent the fish on to Dick in the following afternoon's post (4 October). The carp arrived safely, although as the weather was still rather warm I'm sure Dick 'smelled' it arrive before he actually saw it! One of the first jobs was to take a photograph of the beast, and soon Dick's local fishing friends, Pete Thomas and Bob Rutland, were by his side looking in wonderment at this superb specimen. Before the skinning of the fish was started Dick took several plaster casts. Decomposition had already taken place and the thing was starting to rot! Undeterred by all this the three gentlemen started on the unenviable task. The skin was full of oil and therefore went through two successive degreasing processes

*Work starts in earnest on Bob Richards' fish – Pete Thomas and Bob Rutland with the unenviable task.*

through the good offices of Dick's friend Pat Russell, who was then a director of George W. Russells of Hitchin. A lot of the skin was too decomposed to be retained and had to be cut out, which meant using plastic wood to fill it. The job was completed by Dick Walker who finally hand-finished it to a high standard. Sometime later it went on show at a provincial hobbies exhibition. Dick's local fishing club, Hitchin AC, had mounted a display there and Bob Richard's record carp took pride of place beside some other fine stuffed fish.

Before the end of 1951 other important events transpired, the first of these in November being Bob's election as a member of the Carp Catchers' Club. This club was to become synonymous with major advancements in carp fishing as the 1950s unfolded. Secondly, Bob reported in the club's rotary letter in December of that year that: 'Mrs Barnardiston is to leave Bernithan Court and the place is up for sale.' This then gave leave to the view that any future fishing could be in

jeopardy. However, Mrs Barnardiston informed Bob that she would give the names of people who she had allowed to fish to the new owner – so there was some hope. By April 1952 the auction at which the property was to be sold had taken place, and it failed to sell! Matters were left somewhat in abeyance until news reached both Bob Richards and Dick Walker that indeed the court had a new owner. What's more, this news had originated from Norfolk! There, a dedicated carp fisher of some note who had watched with considerable interest and excitement the events surrounding the capture of Bob Richards' record carp, had wasted no time in contacting an influential friend in Ross-on-Wye. Because newspaper reports had given the pool's name and whereabouts, this carp fisher (named Dick Kingsley-Kefford) had found out through his friend the name of the new owner. The upshot of all this was that Dick Kefford had a permit for himself and a friend to fish Bernithan Court Pool from Friday, 4 July until Sunday, 6 July.

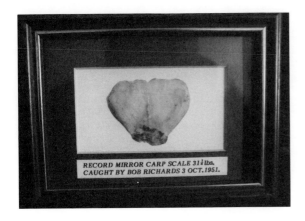

*This scale from Bob Richards' fish is the only known one in a case. It is owned by Mike Wilson.*

## A VINTAGE YEAR

On 20 June Dick Walker and Peter Thomas arrived at the pool, Bob Richards also visiting them on that day. He talked through all he knew of the pool where he had seen fish feeding and, more importantly, where he had caught them. Dick and Peter were taken aback by the beauty of Bernithan, though the weed and algae seemed a major problem and the natural food that abounded in the water drew breath from both anglers. The natural charm of the boat house on the eastern bank and the large willows on the western bank seemed to give the water a perfect balance, yet also gave it a foreboding air.

The size of the water was just right, being some 3 acres in extent, and with its delightful rail the dam had a spillway at one end and a stout fence at the other which, once climbed, gave access to the western bank. All was overgrown with little in the way of a pathway being evident – indeed, once you passed the spot of Bob Richards' triumph to one side of the mighty willows, another clearing marked the point which was as far as you could go. Then, other than hacking through a seemingly impenetrable mass of osier beds which had grown unattended and fallen criss-cross on top of one another, access was difficult. All along this bank the water got shallower, until once past four small islands – situated two-thirds along and close to the bank – the water was just 4ft deep and eventually ended but a few inches deep at the head of the pool where the inlet stream entered.

By contrast the opposite northern bank had a stretch of open, low-lying meadow and some scattered, old pollard willows. Then the lower half of this bank was heavily lined with a mixture of oak, elm and alder trees. High above these stood two balsam poplars in a spot roughly halfway along. The pool seemed to ooze neglect and was obviously a place well suited to carp. Talking of which, Dick and Peter saw plenty of these. They were astounded at the size of the blue-grey shapes that swam through openings in the weed – could they be real, for some seemed impossible and quite beyond their previous experience? We must remember that by then these Leney carp

In early May Dick Kefford wrote to Dick Walker – they had corresponded for some months before this time – telling him not only of his permission to fish, but also that his friend could not now manage the trip after all. Then he further suggested that Dick Walker might like to accompany him instead! Walker wrote an enthusiastic letter back stating that he'd be only too pleased to fish as a guest of Dick Kefford. He also asked if Kefford could furnish the name and present address of the new owner. The name Kefford gave was Col. J. F. Maclean, a gentleman who was then living in the locality but who only moved to the court in the latter half of May 1952.

Dick Walker wrote to J. F. Maclean explaining that he was an experienced and serious angler who would leave the water and surrounding property the way he found it. Walker also mentioned that the small, élite organization of which he was secretary, the Carp Catchers' Club, were always looking for new waters that held carp and, that Bernithan had come highly recommended! The letter Walker received from Maclean was sympathetic to the idea of Dick and a friend fishing for a few days come the start of the season. Dick had now pulled off two visits to what was to become the carp angler's Mecca. I would hazard a guess that his thoughts kept him awake on many a night, for within a month he would tread the banks of a record-breaking water at the start of the momentous 1952 angling season!

*The first weekend of the 1952 season: Pete Thomas's 28-pounder was caught from a swim to the left of the picture and off the dam wall. Just visible close to the willow tree is Walker's rod pointing skywards!*

were fully grown and in the twentieth year of their life. There can be little doubt that some (perhaps three or four) had grown beyond the size of any other carp that swam in England – either then or now! There were so many big fish that Dick's and Pete's conversations lasted all night long as they could only begin to guess as to what they might weigh. They were greatly impressed at the fish they saw, and even on this first visit they saw two absolute monsters and began talking about the possibility of fish in the region of 50–60lb!

The weekend had started with wind and rain, but by the second day the wind had died and the following night all lay calm. The pair were fishing from the dam area as this gave a complete view of the pool's surface and afforded immediate access to the deepest water – around 11ft. A cast made in the dead of night by Pete Thomas put a large piece of bread paste some 30yd out into deep water. His uncluttered presentation of the bait without hindrance of either float or lead lay undisturbed for some hours. It would be almost 4 a.m. before his line ran out to a slow, steady run. Peter had only just remarked to Dick that he would give it 'five minutes more'. It was

a wise move, for as the run came so Peter coolly hit it as he struck through a full ninety degrees. There was a short pause, then off it went with tremendous power. It moved quickly from left to right, surfaced with a magnificent boil and then bore strongly down. There were weedbeds stretching away from both sides of where Pete fished, but luckily the carp at this stage made no attempt to get into them. Having then moved about 30yd it made its first attempt to bore into the weeds. Applying all the pressure he dared, the fish stopped. It did, however, get into some thin weed but with its constant turning and boring the weed just flew off the line. The battle was nearly won, and with Dick Walker at that point on all fours with the big net, the carp slowly wallowed towards it. Before too long and as Peter drew the fish in, Dick gently lifted the net under it. Once in the net the fireworks started, for the carp was far from finished. Dick Walker remembers that it nearly dragged the net with him hanging on into the pool, but he was having none of it, and with much effort he lifted it out of the water by grasping the net's mesh.

Having no scales available that were capable of weighing anything above 16lb, the monster was placed in a large sack and put into Bernithan's deep water. Seven o'clock came and Peter could wait no longer, so off he went to the nearby cottages up on the hill in the hope of finding some suitable scales. Some were found that weighed up to 25lb, but when they were tried the indicator went 'clonk' against the stop! It was a little while later that suitable, accurate scales were found, and the big mirror weighed in at 28lb 10oz. It was the second-largest carp ever landed, and the excitement in both anglers' eyes was hard to hide as the new owner of the court, Col. Maclean (who also saw the carp), cross-examined the two men before they left. As they were leaving, Col. Maclean told them that from then on members of the Carp Catchers' Club could fish the water at any time in the coarse fishing season, providing that they wrote to ask for permission first and that not more than four people would fish there at any one time. The Carp Catchers' Club, of which there were eventually twelve members, for obvious reasons soft-peddled on the number of visits and the number of members present on each occasion. They felt very strongly that they should take far less than full advantage of the colonel's terms. This state of affairs persisted until Col. and Mrs Maclean left Bernithan in the mid-1960s.

Back on the subject of Peter Thomas's mirror carp, it displayed a peculiar mouth which appeared to have slipped under its chin – underslung was how Dick Walker had referred to it. Something happened to this carp that was far from usual. I can reveal some forty years later that the fish was never to see Bernithan again, for Walker and Thomas took the beast away with them. It was wrapped in wet sacks and towels, the plan being to release it into the local village pond at Hitchin! The talk on the journey home was of their good fortune, the size of the monsters they had seen and how they planned to outwit them. With regular interruptions to water the fish, they eventually arrived home. It is sad to report, but the fish did not survive the long ordeal and succumbed soon after being placed into the small pond; it was later buried. It is interesting to note that the report in the *Fishing Gazette* of Saturday 5 July 1952 of Peter Thomas's fish made no mention of Bernithan Court Pool, but merely 'a private lake in the West of England'. This came about not through Dick Walker and colleagues in the Carp Catchers' Club wanting to keep the location quiet, but was rather a stipulation of Col. Maclean that from then on the name was not to be revealed. So how, and more importantly who, thought of the name Redmire? Here we need look no further than B. B. who, because of the surrounding colour of the soil, perfectly described this 'blind' to hide the water's identity. Even today that reddish coloured soil is very much in evidence.

Understandably, two monster carp – one a record-breaker and the other a second best – all within nine months, made the angling world think that the impossible had happened and that lightning had struck twice. But although Redmire had impressed the angling world, it would later startle it.

Barely had Dick Walker returned from Redmire that first week of the season than he was to make a return visit on Friday, 4 July – this time

*Success on the first trip to Redmire – Pete Thomas holds the second largest carp ever caught, a 28lb 10oz mirror.*

*Pete's 28-pounder was removed from Redmire, and is seen here being released into a local pond at Hitchin. Sadly, it did not survive.*

it was the standing arrangement he had with Dick Kefford. Both travelled in some luxury, courtesy no less of Dick Kefford's 18hp Vauxhall Velox. This trip lasted three days but was unfortunate in that no large carp were landed. Dick Kefford did, however, catch a small one, a 5lb 8oz common, proving that Redmire held all sizes of fish at the time.

*Early sunshine forms columns of mist across Redmire. This picture, taken in 1952, clearly shows the old boat house to the right.*

## B. B.'s First Encounter

A few days later, on 9 July, B. B. made his first visit to the pool. This trip lasted four days and was full of drama as B. B. was exposed for the first time to the giants of Bernithan. After this trip he wrote: 'Bernithan holds some truly gigantic fish up to and possibly over 40lb. Most are mirrors, but as we shall learn some huge common carp as well.'

B. B. arrived soon after 7 p.m. on the 9th and met Bob Richards at the bankside. It was a good evening – still and warm – and before dusk he saw two very big fish roll far out. He fished from the dam wall until midnight and Bob fished from the famed Willow pitch, but neither had a bite. They were up and on the job at 3 a.m., fishing until 9 a.m. but still no bites.

After breakfast, B. B. walked up the bank to the islands, these four small islets being but a short hop from the bank and two-thirds along the western bank. Once there he saw a huge mirror in the shallow water upending and feeding. He slipped back for his rod but when he returned the fish had departed in a cloud of mud. By then the sun was very hot and B. B. decided on a 'recce' of the pool to learn something of its bottom. Opposite the islands he found the lake bed to be clear of weed and having a depth of 5–6ft. Further along this eastern bank he found a carp hole which he immediately named 'the bottomless

*B.B. – Denys Watkins-Pitchford – fishing from the punt in front of Redmire's small islands in July 1952.*

pit'. It was situated just above the boat house which was in good repair during the first few years that the Carp Catchers' Club fished there. B. B.'s theory on the bottomless pit is worth recording here: 'It might have been the site of a tree which grew there and which was pulled out by the works when the pool was made.' He also saw another monster carp in this spot and he was sure that this was its lair, for it was evident throughout the period of his visit and leaped out several times.

Returning to the dam area he found the pool's bed thick with weed growth, but further out where Peter Thomas caught his fish it was clear. By far the biggest problem B. B. and Bob Richards faced on this trip was the floating weed which the wind constantly moved about like an ice pack, especially when the westerly wind blew stronger. Above the islands this weed was far less thickly distributed and the hard, clear bottom could be seen. It was when B. B. elected to alight in the punt later that day that he saw the greatest number of carp as well as one big common carp. This 30lb-category fish swam cleverly under the craft, and when B. B. looked down he saw the fish's back which reminded him of the criss-cross pattern of chicken wire.

The following day, after another uneventful night, B. B. decided to fish from the punt in the clear area up on the shallows, having first groundbaited this area with 'dough'. He saw two carp come close to the punt – a mirror well over 20lb and a smaller one. They moved slowly around the general area and then the big one swam round the hookbait and eventually took it! A short run made B. B. reach for his rod, but before he could strike the fish spat out the bait. His next run came later that evening from the same spot but about 30yd further out – a big fish had been rolling in this spot all evening. About 10 p.m. all went quiet and he sensed something was about to happen. He had 2yd of line coiled on the punt floor. Unfortunately, at that moment the entire Higgs family from the cottage arrived with much noise and vibration. B. B. turned to young Eric to tell him to keep quiet when he heard the line go 'ping'. Whipping his head

around he saw the coiled line had all gone – the fish had felt the jar of the reel and had left it, thereby depriving B. B. of the chance of a carp. This was shocking bad luck on his part as it turned out to be one of the few chances B. B. ever had in his time at Bernithan, but it did provide high drama as he came to the end of his first visit. Bob Richards also had a dry net during this visit, something that all the members of the Carp Catchers' Club suffered for most of the time they fished at the pool.

Within a couple of weeks and towards the middle of July, Bernithan drew Dick Walker back, this time with his companion Bernard Venables. Bernard was a successful carp catcher in his own right and was later elected to the Carp Catchers' Club. This trip lasted a couple of days but produced no fish on the bank, although Dick did hook an absolute monster. There were some very big fish visible just cruising up and down in the middle, and he cast out a crust with a running rig so that the crust floated up above the lead to the surface, right out in the middle. An enormous carp (he thought it weighed about 60lb) came along and took the crust with the greatest of confidence, but spat it out again before he could tighten up the big angle between hook and lead, and lead and rod. It's interesting to note here that the largest fish seen were growing ever bigger with each trip to the pool – remember that these were experienced men and in Dick Walker's case he had already handled two big fish from the pool and was getting his eye in, so to speak. The fishes' estimated average size grew even more as the years went by, so read on.

Later in July Dick Walker went again to Redmire, this time with Maurice Ingham. Both men settled in for the night, and both were using an earlier pattern of electric bite alarm in which the line was held between two contacts, keeping them separate until the line was pulled out. All was quiet until suddenly at around 3 a.m. a check on a reel shrieked out. It was Dick's special multiplier outfit (his second rod) and a large crust had been taken. Dick struck but found the line disappearing up round his legs! A great big rat had taken the crust, hooked fair and square, and had tried to escape. It provided light relief to the two fishermen who were tensed up at the thought of a Bernithan monster drawing ever closer to the baited hook.

A little time later Maurice's alarm went off – apparently the fish had dropped the bait – then the alarm went off again and then stopped again. Maurice told Dick later that these indications were a series of small pulls which continued until 3.30 a.m. when the line ran out steadily. Maurice struck, the rod making a tremendous 'whoosh' in the calm night air. He called out to Dick, 'Fish on.' The fish made a thunderous splashing directly opposite Walker and great ripples spread along the bank. Maurice waded out into the darkness, mainly to keep himself between the fish and the willows. He then said to Dick, 'Go and get some stones.'

It took Dick perhaps two or three minutes to find some stones. In the meantime, however, the fish had tried several times to pass him, but each time sidestrain, combined with splashing, turned it back into the lake. Walker's stones were not needed as the fish was now under control, but it was some time before Maurice's rod indicated that the fish was nearing the bank. Dick was kneeling beside Maurice, some corrugated iron

saving him from getting wet feet, and soon Maurice had the fish ready for netting. Dick made no mistake as a great mirror carp wallowed over the net. He hauled it to the side, got hold of the net's mesh and heaved the whole lot up the bank and well away from the water's edge. Maurice followed with a lamp and soon they were back at the tent site. There they removed the hook, which was well embedded in the mouth, and weighed the fish roughly at just short of 25lb. What a grand carp this was and a well-deserved one – a fitting triumph for a great carp angler. Later in the day it was weighed in exactly at 24lb 12oz. Actually, it was later found that the spring balance from which this fish was hung was inaccurate so that it really weighed an ounce or two over 25lb. However, neither Maurice nor anyone else cared two hoots about setting the record straight.

With both of Dick's friends, Peter Thomas and now Maurice, capturing 20lb-plus carp, Dick must have asked himself when his chance would come. As it turned out he didn't have to wait long – in fact, just two days!

Dick and Maurice left Bernithan to go to the famous Dagenham Lake in Essex, home of many big carp since the War. It was here that Dick caught his very first twenty-pounder, a wonderful 22lb 12oz common carp.

*Maurice Ingham with the fish of his dreams, caught from Redmire in July 1952 – 24lb 12oz.*

To say that carp fishing was reaching new heights would be an understatement. Members of the Carp Catchers' Club were starting to reap the benefits of combining their considerable knowledge to further the understanding of the carp's habits, the conditions that affected their quarry, and how and why they fed at certain times. But as increasingly successful as they were, none of them – Dick Walker included – was quite prepared for what was about to happen as August slipped into September. The realization of what Bernithan held and to what size the little Leney fish had grown, combined with what the Carp Catchers' Club members knew was likely to happen was indeed about to happen.

### The Carp Catchers' Club Carp

On Friday, 12 September 1952 Peter Thomas and Dick Walker again went to Bernithan. The account of what transpired on this visit is a timeless classic that has been recounted and covered in a dozen or more volumes – but never has this version appeared until now.

I publish here Dick Walker's personal verbal account given live and recorded at a British Carp Study Group evening I had the good fortune to organize back in 1972 at Golders Green in London. This is Dick's never-to-be-forgotten story of how Clarissa the common carp broke the record right out of sight.

'It's a pretty simple story to tell, but before I start on it I want to make it quite clear that although at the time I didn't think I was exactly a slouch at carp fishing, catching that record fish and indeed catching any record fish was very much a matter of luck.

'Peter and I went to Redmire and we had some adventures on the way – two flat tyres and trouble with the chassis. We arrived in pouring rain and pitched a tent. It was the darkest night I can ever remember, so that we didn't get off to a very good start, but the most interesting thing perhaps about the whole business was that at that time Pete and I were fishing with absolutely identical tackle. Same hooks, same line, same reel and same rods, and we were fishing the same place with the rods in rests within a foot of one another. The baits were out in the water in about 12ft or thereabouts, again within a matter of a few feet

*Dick Walker's carp fishing set-up, similar to that used when he landed the record 44lb common carp. Note the 'clip' bite alarm (just in front of the lamp) and the 36in triangular landing net.*

of one another: we cast them out into the dark, but the 'plops' seemed to be in about the same place. So right away I want to say that it was just an even chance whether the carp took my bait or Pete Thomas's, and I'm sure if it had taken Pete's it would have been landed a fair bit more skilfully and perhaps a good deal more quickly than actually happened. We knew pretty well where we wanted to be fishing: it was on the edge of the drop-off. Anyone who knows Redmire will understand why I say that, because the bank shelves fairly slowly at first and then drops off much more quickly to the old river bed – the river bed of the Garron which was dammed up to make the pool.

'Where we were fishing the dam was about 20yd down the bank to our right and we were casting out parallel to the dam. On each side of our pitch there were big weedbeds stretching out I suppose 20–25yd. That's all gone now – the pool changes every year – but there was this dense weedbed on the right and another one on the left going on and past beyond the willow trees. It was clearly going to be necessary if you got stuck into a big fish to try and beat it out in the open middle of the pool and not try to bring it to the bank or near the bank until it was sufficiently tired for you to have some control over it.

'We realized this before we started to fish. We cast out, and in those days we were using simple 'clip' contact bite alarms, the sort you clip the line between two contacts which holds them apart: when the line gets pulled out the buzzer goes, and keeps on going until you switch it off. We sat fishing until about a quarter to six and then I had a run on mine. Line was trickling out very slowly indeed. In fact, I wasn't sure it was trickling out until I put the back of my hand up under the rod between the butt ring and the reel and I could feel it slowly slithering. I remember it tickling the hairs on the back of my hand. But of course you can get just as eerie a feeling with a 4lb carp as you can with a 40lb carp! I had no idea what had taken it and I did all the usual things: put the pick-up in – in those days we had the old 'claw'-type pick-up, not a bail arm, so it was always necessary to discipline oneself to make

sure the line had been picked up properly and wasn't twice round the pick-up or missed altogether or something.

'So, I checked that, very cool…shouldn't have been so cool if I'd known what had the bait, perhaps. I hit this thing and for the next six or seven minutes there was the most curious kind of sensation in playing this fish. I put a fair bit of stick on it, but not as much as was possible – you let a fish declare itself unless there's reason to stop it, and there was not then because, as I say, I did not want it to come near yet. From then on for the next perhaps ten minutes or so it felt just as if someone had filled an old sock with wet sand and hit the top of the rod as hard as they could. I mean, I've not got feeble wrists by any means, and I was holding the rod butt almost, though not quite, vertical and this pull was so savage that it slammed the rod tip almost down to the water. And it kept happening every six or seven seconds, this frightful sort of crunching feeling, and I really didn't know what was happening.

'I had all sorts of thoughts like "Have I foulhooked something by the tail?" or "Is this some kind of fish other than a carp?" It was very weird, I've caught a lot of carp in my time but I've never had this enormous thump before. I think the fish had got his head more or less vertically down and was trying to drive into the bottom and hitting the line with his tail. When you get a fish over 3ft long, and with the power of a carp swinging its tail as hard as it can, you are liable to get a bit of a thump. I knew it must be a good big fish because anything under about 10lb usually takes off fast and you can exercise some control – you've only got to stop it – but this thing was going very slowly. I should not think it was going more than half a mile an hour towards the dam.

'Now, all along the dam at Redmire there used to be alder trees and they were felled but the roots were still sticking out of the dam like a Medusa's hair, a real bunch of snakes all in the water. I thought, "If it gets in that, whatever it is, it will probably tie me up and I shall lose it." I would always, whatever kind of fishing I'm doing, rather be broken trying to stop a fish than having to break myself after a fish has got tangled up. So I gave it all the stick I could; I won't say I pointed the rod straight at it, but I can remember feeling the corks actually bending under my hands and that meant the rod was pretty well bent.

'After all these thumps I was quite surprised to be able to stop the fish as easily as I did. Once that heavy strain came on it stopped and then it turned to the right which means it was coming along parallel to the dam, partly towards me, and buried itself in the weedbed.

'Peter Thomas...he's a quiet chap, he said: "Tied up in the weeds?" or something like that, and I said, "I think so." Pete then said: "Take it easy, I think you've got a big fish on there" – Pete's a very calm chap! So I said: "I think I'll try hand-lining it," and I pointed the rod straight at where I thought the fish was. But you've got to remember this was pitch-black, I couldn't see the weedbed, I couldn't see the dam, the only thing that was possible to see was just the faint silhouettes of the trees on the opposite bank.

'Anyway, I pointed the rod more or less down the line and gave two or three tugs and this shifted the fish. It went out again in the middle channel and this time it kept coming up to the left, still doing these almighty thumps. It got opposite and then it seemed...I won't say to give up, but at any rate, it had very little more to say about the whole proceedings. I bent the rod into it, and the carp came grudgingly. It went a little way this way, a little way that way, but eventually we got it close enough so it was more or less under the rod. Then Pete shone a big lantern on it and even then I couldn't tell how big it was because here was a fish, an all-scaled common carp – in fact, Pete said: "Oh, it's a common carp" – in a circle of light, and nothing else to measure it by. It was obviously a big fish, but at the time I remember thinking it might be a twenty-pounder; in those days twenty-pounders were not so common as nowadays. None of us had much ambition to do much better than 20lb.

'It rolled about on its side for perhaps thirty seconds or so, then it righted itself, pointing slightly to my right, and it shot under the bank. On the bank at that point there's a bramble bush, and when I say a bramble bush I don't mean three or four strands; this was a great mass of brambles that have died, then new growth and so on. This made a kind of barrier in the water, and under this the bank was rather hollowed out. It crashed through these brambles – I remember hearing the dead brambles from years gone by splinter as it shot in. So, now I was connected to a fish that was almost under my feet, and a bit to the right, and that's a hard situation to deal with because you're trying to sort of push a fish out with the tip of the rod, and rods aren't very well designed for that. Pete said "Take it easy." He laid face-down on this great mass of brambles – how many thorns he must have got in his chest and other vital parts I can't think – with the landing net in one hand which was different from the ones that are used nowadays – a big, triangular net with 3ft arms and a very large bag. He clamped it over the hole that the fish had made and then he called to me to take the torch, then he felt underneath way down along the line. The fish had got its head pointing under the bank and he simply pushed its head around, sort of feeling between the landing net and the brambles – or so he tells me – and pushed the fish's head outwards. The fish must have then thought, "I'm pointing the right way for safety" and shot out, and of course it shot straight into the landing net.

'I then remember Pete having some considerable difficulty in lifting the thing. I still didn't know how big it was because we still had nothing to measure it by. We laid it on the bank. I thought, "This is a hell of a big carp," but I had no idea it was a record one at that time. Pete shone the light down its throat and I got a bit of stick, and cut a little V in the end to act as a disgorger. However, when we looked down the throat, the hook was never in over the barb, just the point was against the roof of the mouth and stopped by the bone. If the line had ever gone slack the hook would have fallen out – it might have caught somewhere else, but it certainly wasn't a secure hookhold. So I poked the hook out, then we put the thing in a sack and hung it up in a spring balance and it pulled that to the stop; that was a 32lb balance. So we took some of the weight on a 16lb balance and got a rough

*Here it is…Dick Walker is all smiles as he holds the massive 44-pounder. Pete Thomas's battered old car can be seen in the background.*

figure of 41lb 8oz. There the matter rested as far as the weight was concerned until it got properly weighed at the London Zoo which was late the next day.

'Sometime about 9 a.m. or thereabouts the next morning I went up to big house and asked if I could use the phone. I rang the London Zoo and said, "Do you want a 40lb carp?" They said, "We've got a 14lb carp," and then I said, "Not a 14lb carp – a *40lb* carp!" The man at the other end made some terse comments about how he did wish hoaxers would think of something better to do on a Saturday morning. Then I had to put it fairly bluntly. I said, "Now look, I say this carp is over 40lb and I've got it here and you can have it if you like. If you don't want it I'm sure Bristol Zoo would be glad to have it and they would not have so far to come. If you send out a vehicle and something to fetch this fish in and you find it's a hoax – all right you've wasted a journey, but if you *don't* send it out and your employers at the Zoological Society find somebody else has got the carp because you wouldn't believe me, I think you might be in worse trouble. Suit yourself, but you must tell me now which it is you are going to do." So he said. "I'll send for it." About six hours later a van arrived with a tub and two obviously unbelieving people

*Pete Thomas supports the magnificent 44lb common. The length was later estimated at 36in from nose to fork of the tail!*

*Clarissa's tremendous girth is shown clearly in this picture taken on Pete Thomas's Box Brownie.*

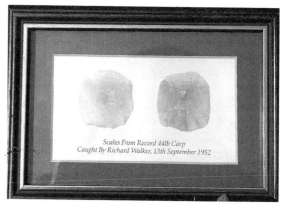

*Scales from Clarissa – property of the author.*

who thought it was going to be a hoax. They were quite surprised to find it wasn't and drove off with the thing.

'Then I sent a telegram to Bernard Venables – because this was the day of the all-England match of that year – which simply said: "Caught carp, 41lb." So that started things moving as far as Bernard Venables and the *Daily Mirror* was concerned. He got Ken Sutton – who was one of the founders of *Angling Times* – to go along to the zoo and collect an inspector of weights and measures on the way so the fish could be weighed without anybody ever having any doubt in the future about the actual weight.

'I was quite surprised to find that they made it 44lb – because our two balances together only made it 41lb 8oz. I did check up to see whether they had included a wet sack or not, but it turned out they hadn't – it was all done properly. So this is going to be one of the few record fish where there has never been any doubt about what it really did weigh.'

## Changing Attitudes

In all honesty this capture can claim to have turned the heads of the nation – never mind those of anglers – through Dick's foresight in installing the carp in London Zoo. It was true, and all and sundry could see it for themselves. The effect this had on angling was considerable. For a start, angling clubs could see that carp didn't need fifty years or more to grow into a worthwhile size. Secondly, *they could be caught* – The Carp Catchers' Club methods had proved that time and time again. In the case of Dick Walker's 44lb carp, the establishment could hardly believe this fish, even though Dick had gone into print during the summer of 1952 saying that 40lb carp existed. Indeed, Dick, Bob Richards, Pete Thomas and Maurice Ingham had all hooked and lost potential record breakers at Bernithan during the course of the summer. To bring matters to a head, as luck would have it the very week that Dick caught the record carp there appeared sceptical letters in the angling press concerning Dick's earlier claims as to the size of carp that grew in British waters. It

was very much 'I told you so,' and I can't help feeling that Dick felt some satisfaction with the capture of the record fish. Straight away Dick and Pete Thomas gave the beast a name – Ravioli after the cold tins of this pasta dish Dick and Pete ate, especially at Bernithan. However, a reporter from a London evening newspaper had different ideas and came up with the name Clarissa. That's the name which stuck.

The most important point Dick was quick to make was that this carp was the Carp Catchers' Club carp. At the time Dick said, 'One hand had caught it, but more than one mind had brought its downfall.' The inevitability of Walker catching this carp was expressed by more than one member of the CCC, but Dick in his unashamed style would have none of it. However, as we have seen in his own account, Dick truly believed luck played a big part in that carp coming to the bank, and indeed the vital part Pete Thomas played cannot be overstated.

So far I have had little to say about the record carp itself. It was a perfect common carp in tiptop health, and a comparative rarity for Bernithan – in fact, very few 'all scalers' came through from the Surrey Trout Farm. This was because the Galician strain of king carp tended to produce the mirror and leather variety for eighty per cent of the time. Although we know fifty carp were stocked into Bernithan, Donald Leney stated that 'Few all scalers were present.' Unfortunately, however, we don't know how *few* made up the Bernithan stocking.

In the excitement of it all Dick and Pete Thomas omitted to measure the record breaker, but Dick stated afterwards that working out with callipers against known objects within the pictures, the length and girth were as follows: length 37in; girth 31in. He thought these figures were only likely to be ½in out either way. So, here was a 3ft-long carp that displayed tremendous width at the shoulders and was 'thick' for the whole length of the body. When Pete Thomas took a picture of Clarissa lying on the ground at Bernithan you will no doubt become aware of the bulk of this carp – all in all it represented a huge fish.

*Clarissa being treated for a small growth on her snout while in captivity at London Zoo, circa 1953.*

A scale from Clarissa's flank was sent to Percy Austin who had a vast amount of experience of scale reading. He gave the verdict that the fish was aged fifteen years. Indeed, he had also read scales from Bob Richards' carp and Pete Thomas' 28lb 10oz mirror, both of which he was certain were fourteen years old. At the time, these estimations actually gave rise to a false impression of the age of the fish. Further evidence, first revealed in the mid-1970s by Kevin Clifford and Len Arbery, showed that all the scale annual rings showed was how long the fish grew for, not how old it was. This meant that all three carp mentioned were from the original stocking of 1934. The carp at Bernithan did, of course, spawn, for the anglers often found carp about 2in long in large numbers in the weeds in summer. Maurice Ingham took some of them home and kept them in a tank in his house for quite a long time. It was very noticeable that in the season following the appearance of large numbers of these little carp, there were always considerable numbers of fish in the region of 1½–2lb in weight, which could be caught with float tackle. An important point comes in here: it is significant that every single one that was caught – these captures run into dozens – had common carp scaling. In fact, people like Dick Walker cannot remember ever catching or hearing about anybody else catching a carp weighing under 10lb which was not of this form. It is therefore fair to assume that most, if not all of the mirror and leather types in Bernithan were from the fifty initial carp.

Perhaps the most important factor after the 44-pounder was landed was Dick sending it to the London Zoo. It certainly aroused interest in the angling world, and expanded the interest in carp fishing to the extent that club officials and committee members were under pressure from club members to stock with carp. The importance of gravel pits as future angling venues was coming to the fore, primarily as a spin-off from the massive building programme Britain undertook in the 1950s – sand and gravel were needed in vast quantities.

But back to Bernithan or, as it was renamed in late 1952 by B. B., Redmire Pool. It's not hard to see why this pseudonym was chosen, for the soil in the region of Ross-on-Wye is of this reddy hue. It was J. F. Maclean who had asked that the whereabouts of the pool should not be revealed from the start of the fishing in 1952. Until the name Redmire was released, the lake was simply known as a private lake in the 'West of England'. So, 1952 ended and the grand total of carp from Redmire could be counted:

| **Dick Walker** | 22 June | 5lb (2) |
| | 24 August | 7lb |
| | 13 September | 44lb |
| | 14 September | 6lb 12oz |
| **Pete Thomas** | 21 June | 8lb 12oz |
| | 23 June | 28lb 10oz |
| **Maurice Ingham** | 30 July | 24lb 12oz |
| **Dick Kefford** | 7 July | 5lb 12oz |

These nine carp represented only a part of the total number hooked, for the problem of hooked fish coming adrift was a bigger headache than actually getting runs from Redmire carp! This meant that out of every four runs that were struck, and apparently struck successfully, three came to nothing through the fish shedding the hook at the end of its first run. Dick Walker stated in later years:

'I now realize that a number of opportunities were probably lost because, in general, we all tended to wait for a positive run. I think that we might have hooked more carp had we struck at small indications, but we were reluctant to do so because we felt strongly that unless you were fairly sure that you would hook a fish, it was better not to strike as fruitless striking tended to make the fish more suspicious and they were suspicious enough, God knows, as it was. I do think though that we should have experimented a great deal more with some kind of more sensitive bite indication.'

The main bait tried at Redmire was bread in one form or the other, although Dick Walker came up with an ingenious variation of bread paste and bread crust together. It was named balanced crust and consisted of crust on the bend of the hook with enough paste moulded round the hookshank to make it just sink. The bait would always sit upright in the water with the crust uppermost. An added benefit was that the line would come away from *under* the bait so it would lie flat along the bottom. The Carp Catchers' Club were well aware of the potential that lay in using finer or more supple line, and Dick had experimented with and actually used braided nylon when he caught the record fish.

## Tackle Development

The development of tackle produced with carp in mind in particular goes back before Redmire was heard of, but showed its worth when these really big fish were encountered. Again it was Dick Walker at the helm, although he had much help and advice from his fellow carp catchers. Dick actually worked out and then hand-built some of the revolutionary tackle developments that were to see success not only at Redmire, and which were to become standard issue to all potential carp fishers. Also, after World War II tackle development and manufacture not surprisingly saw something of a recovery.

Resuming his carp-catching activities at this time, Dick Walker started to catch bigger and better carp, but all too often the inadequacies of his tackle became further highlighted. Rods in particular were an area that seemed badly catered for. Dick wrote to both Hardy's and Allcock's

with the idea of producing a rod specially for carp fishing – they wrote back saying there was no real demand for such a weapon! However, Maj. Courtney Williams, a Director of Allcock's, did send some choice bamboo, suggesting to Dick that he made his own rod. That's just what Dick did, first designing and then making one of his own. This marks the commencement of the first purpose-built carp rod ever made.

Dick calculated what the correct tapers would be for a 10ft two-piece split-cane rod, and made up a rod with a test curve of some 20oz which was called the Mk II. Experience with this led him to think that a little extra stiffness was needed, and another rod was made, this time using double-built split cane – the Mk III. However, it was found that double building added more weight

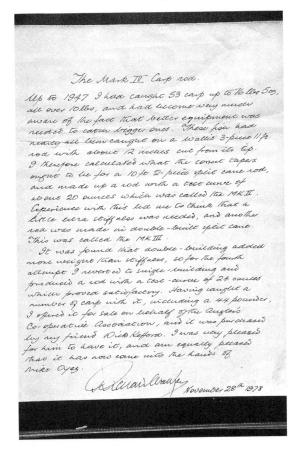

*Hand-written account by Dick Walker of the development of the purpose-built carp rod.*

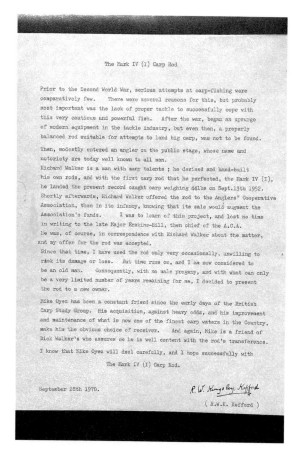

The Mark IV (I) Carp Rod

Prior to the Second World War, serious attempts at carp-fishing were comparatively few. There were several reasons for this, but probably most important was the lack of proper tackle to successfully cope with this very cautious and powerful fish. After the war, began an upsurge of modern equipment in the tackle industry, but even then, a properly balanced rod suitable for attempts to land big carp, was not to be found.

Then, modestly entered an angler on the public stage, whose name and notoriety are today well known to all men.

Richard Walker is a man with many talents ; he devised and hand-built his own rods, and with the first carp rod that he perfected, the Mark IV (I), he landed the present record caught carp weighing 44lbs on Sept.13th 1952. Shortly afterwards, Richard Walker offered the rod to the Anglers' Cooperative Association, then in its infancy, knowing that its sale would augment the Association's funds.     I was to learn of this project, and lost no time in writing to the late Major Erskine-Hill, then chief of the A.C.A. He was, of course, in correspondence with Richard Walker about the matter, and my offer for the rod was accepted.

Since that time, I have used the rod only very occasionally, unwilling to risk its damage or loss.  But time runs on, and I am now considered to be an old man.   Consequently, with no male progeny, and with what can only be a very limited number of years remaining for me, I decided to present the rod to a new owner.

Mike Oyez has been a constant friend since the early days of the British Carp Study Group.  His acquisition, against heavy odds, and his improvement and maintenance of what is now one of the finest carp waters in the Country, make him the obvious choice of receiver.   And again, Mike is a friend of Dick Walker's who assures me he is well content with the rod's transference.

I know that Mike Oyez will deal carefully, and I hope successfully with The Mark IV (I) Carp Rod.

September 28th 1978.

*R. W. Kingsley. Kefford.*

( R.W.K. Kefford )

*Dick Kingsley-Kefford's letter confirming the authenticity and ownership of 'Mark IV No 1' (now the property of the author).*

than stiffness, so for the fourth attempt he reverted to single building. During the winter of 1950/1 he produced a rod with a test curve of 1½lb which proved satisfactory – the Mk IV.

The technical ramifications this rod was to have through its excellent design has a bearing on fishing rods that are made to this day. Dick, after discussions with others, had used his not inconsiderable mathematical skills to 'compute' where the stress points and subsequent increase in diameter was needed. The term Dick used was 'compound taper', and as far as I know this principle had been little used before. He also introduced another word into the carp-fishing vernacular – test curve. The Mk IV rod boasted a 1½lb test curve, which meant that it bent into a

quarter-curve with a pull of 1½lb. This loading meant that the rod would handle leads up to 1oz and was suitable for lines in the 6–12lb range This actual rod, of which I am the fortunate keeper, is as straight as the day Dick made it, the through action/compound taper makes it feel like a deceptively easy action weapon, but put a bend in it and gradually you feel the power coming through. Its long-casting qualities were used by Dick to great effect while perch fishing on Arlesey Lake, many of the big perch Dick caught that winter coming to the original Mk IV.

Because of the Mk IV's success, Dick made more during 1951 and 1952 – the second was destined for B. B., the third for Bernard Venables, the fourth for Bob Richards and the fifth for his long-time angling companion Peter Thomas. The final seal of the Mk IV's prowess came when Dick landed the record 44lb fish on his original model.

With the public awareness Dick and his friends aroused, it was inevitable that he would be approached by a manufacturer interested in the rod, but he had no time for the big companies – after all, he had given them the chance years before. It was through Dick's contact with Ken Sutton – one of the founders of *Angling Times* – that he met Jim Bruce (known as Jimmy James). Bruce was the proprietor of B. James & Son of West Ealing. They were a small, independent rod-making firm, but with a good reputation. After consultations and after Walker had tested several prototype versions, the B. James & Son, Richard Walker Mk IV carp rod came on to the market in early 1953. On the first batch, some twenty rods, Dick actually signed the butt in Indian ink as inspected and passed by himself. Slightly later when Dick knew he could trust Jimmy James's work, a transfer of his signature was added. The man who made most if not all of these early models was Bob Southwell, a master rod builder who rates as probably the finest split-cane maker of all time. After working for James for a number of years Southwell bought a tackle business at Croydon in Surrey called 'The Captain' and started to produce in small quantities only first-class Mk IVs from these premises.

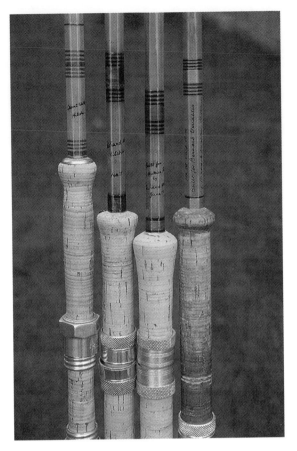

*Four hand-built Richard Walker carp rods, the Mk IV rod which subdued the record 44lb common is the second from the left.*

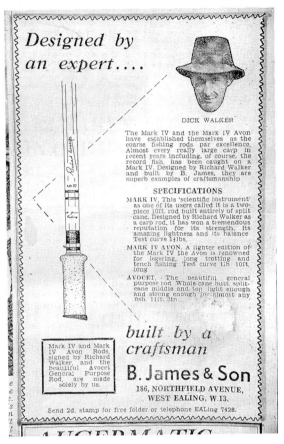

Designed by
an expert....

DICK WALKER

The Mark IV and the Mark IV Avon have established themselves as the coarse fishing rods par excellence. Almost every really large carp in recent years including, of course, the record fish, has been caught on a Mark IV. Designed by Richard Walker and built by B. James, they are superb examples of craftsmanship

SPECIFICATIONS

MARK IV. This 'scientific instrument' as one of its users called it is a two-piece 10ft. rod built entirely of split cane. Designed by Richard Walker as a carp rod, it has won a tremendous reputation for its strength. Its amazing lightness and its balance Test curve 1½lbs.

MARK IV AVON. A lighter edition of the Mark IV the Avon is renowned for legering, long trotting and tench fishing Test curve 1lb 10ft. long

AVOCET. The beautiful general purpose rod Whole cane butt, split-cane middle and top light enough and strong enough for almost any fish 11ft. 3in.

Mark IV and Mark IV Avon Rods, signed by Richard Walker, and the beautiful Avocet General Purpose Rod, are made solely by us.

*built by a*
*craftsman*
B. James & Son
186, NORTHFIELD AVENUE,
WEST EALING, W.13.
Send 2d. stamp for free folder or telephone EALing 7428.

*Early B. James & Son advert.*

On the reel front, the Hardy Altex range of fixed-spool models, (available in three sizes) were a well-built power-house type of reel. All had a narrow (front to back) spool which inhibited casting quite badly, but they did boast the 'full bail arm', a patent that Hardy relinquished only in 1954. The J. W. Young ambidex was a good, affordable fixed-spool reel (unlike the Altex which was rather expensive). Another famous fixed-spool reel of the period – and one Walker used for carp fishing – was the Felton Crosswind made by Allcock's. This quite bizarre looking reel had a most peculiar reciprocating action which moved the spool around in an undulating action to stop the line digging in. This is the reel Dick Walker suggested to Maurice Ingham when

Maurice wrote to Walker following his two-part 'How to catch carp' articles published in *The Fishing Gazette* of September 1949.

However the mighty Mitchell fixed-spool reel from France soon came to the fore, Walker being one of the first who quickly saw the advantages of this now famous and long-standing model. The method of carp fishing Dick Walker employed called for a resistance-free set-up, the fish moving off with the bait and not realizing it was attached to anything. But fishing at night – which Dick did often – meant that you had to try to stay awake while watching silver paper or a white-painted stick laid over the line. Walker was the one who 'invented' the electric bite indicator. The initial version held the line between two contacts, the box that held the components being placed between the reel and first ring. When the line was pulled from the contacts the circuit closed, and with that a buzzer sounded and a small light came on. Very ingenious. The rod was placed in a special shaped rod rest to allow free passage of the line and with the top of the rest often painted white to give visibility in darker conditions. A purpose-made carp hook had yet to be made, but Walker and his followers used the Allcock's Model Perfect in sizes 4 and 2.

So ended the momentous 1952 season, the Carp Catchers' Club year – but could they do it again?

## WEED, WEED AND MORE WEED

As time drew close to the start of the 1953 season the excitement mounted for those lucky enough to fish Redmire, and the expectations on what might be caught were especially high for B. B. and Bob Richards. They were to fish the first two days of the new season, but with the weather being somewhat indifferent they thought their chances were going to be poor.

The sight that greeted them as the pool came into view made the two anglers gasp. Bob Richards, who'd last seen the pool some months before, could hardly believe his eyes for nearly the whole surface was choked solid with weed. Not only that, but the accumulated scum was the worst he had ever seen – it appeared to be several inches thick! The only free areas were a few yards out from the dam over the deepest water and in the far shallows.

Fishing for the first night, neither man had a touch and Redmire was unusually quiet with no gigantic splashes from the big fish. As soon as it got light, B. B. spotted a large object floating in the weeds at the top end in the shallows. Bob and B. B. boarded the punt and slowly made their way along the length of Redmire. Once close to it, they realized that it was obviously a very dead big carp. The corpse displayed itself as being full of spawn and gas, and as it was too big to get into the punt it was manoeuvred by careful work

towards the bank. It was simply a matter then of hauling it ashore.

Puncturing the flank of the fish to let the gas out (and standing upwind), the fish was weighed accurately on Bob Richards' scales which registered 38lb. Why it had died was a mystery, but as fish perished through the rigours of spawning at the pool every now and then, maybe this was one? B. B. took a scale from the carp and this was subsequently sent to Dick Walker who read it at 15 years plus, the same as his record fish. As we have already seen with the benefit of hindsight, we know scale reading gives only information on the growing cycle and not the age. The likelihood was that this carp was an original from the 1934 stocking, and it is probably fair to say that a number had succumbed at various times through the previous twenty years. This incident aside, very little more happened and certainly no runs were forthcoming. Bob and B. B. left a little disappointed with what had seemed at the outset a golden opportunity.

Within a few days the pool saw anglers again. This time they were in the shape of the Dagenham carp catcher Harry Grief, who brought a guest from Dagenham with him named George Piper. They were greeted by Bob Richards and all three fished for a further two days, again to no avail. The year 1953 was to be a most difficult one for outwitting the Redmire carp, and it seems that the weed played havoc with all attempts to present a bait correctly. July came, and another good angler by the name of Bob Rutland tried his hand at the carp – his account at the time showed that the weed was getting worse and he too came away fishless. Although no runs came his way he did, however, see sights that stayed within his mind for years. His description of some of the fish he saw makes you shiver:

'That first visit was memorable for many reasons, none more than the extraordinary sized carp I saw. Having seen Dick Walker's carp in the zoo I have no hesitation in saying that Redmire held carp far larger than the record. One afternoon I saw cruising in the vicinity of the boat house a monstrous mirror carp that must have been at least 10lb better than Dick's monster. The tackle I was using, a special carp rod, 12lb line and a size 3 hook, seemed rather inadequate.'

Come the middle of August and B. B. made another trip, this time taking his long-time friend Michael Shepard as a guest. Both nights were ideal – close and still – although with a full moon B. B. thought the likelihood of a bite was rather diminished. Yet again the Redmire monsters were on the prowl. His vivid recollections of 15 August, the first day of his visit, were recounted some years later:

'The largest carp ever came half-out of the water in the pool's centre, its size was unbelievable and I put it well over 50lb and possibly over 60lb. It appeared as big as a small rowing boat! I had a good view as it came out in full view and surged along the surface. I knew there were giants in Redmire but this fish was beyond belief – so there's still every chance of getting something really staggering out of the water.'

A week later Dick Walker and Pete Thomas fished for a few days. Dick hooked a big carp, only to lose it through the hook coming away (again). This run came from the Willow pitch, the scene of his previous triumph. This pitch also turned up the *only* carp to be caught at Redmire for the whole season – it fell to Maurice Ingham and weighed 9lb 8oz.

With the approach of September 1953 Bob Richards was more determined than ever to catch another Redmire carp – after all it was approaching two years since his last. He fished for four days and nights with a friend Vincent Pole, but yet again those carp steadfastly refused to feed. It was to be the last visit by anyone that year and marked a poor season at the pool; after the high spots of 1952 it all seemed so different. Although it was a poor season at Redmire, the carp angler's Mecca, it also turned out to be a very unproductive year for big carp throughout the UK. Just one carp was reported over 20lb, and was caught by Gerry Berth-Jones from the famous Dagenham water at Becontree.

By now thousands of British anglers had visited the London Zoo Aquarium to see its star attraction – Dick Walker's record carp Clarissa. Dick's name was hot property during 1953, for not only did he have his much acclaimed book *Still-Water Angling* (MacGibbon and Kee) published, he also became a regular columnist in the new weekly newspaper for anglers, *The Angling Times*. He had plenty to say on almost all aspects of freshwater angling, though most of his mail bag at the time was made up with questions related to carp. The sudden upsurge of interest in carp fishing also meant that Donald Leney's *Surrey Trout Farm* was to become more busy – indeed, he started to advertise the fact that carp from his farm had grown into record breakers in less than twenty years, and that he was able to supply carp from the same source as the Redmire fish. His trade in carp expanded during this period and it is these fish which provided the legends that are covered elsewhere in this book!

**Solving Problems**

With only one Redmire carp caught during the 1953 season and several big carp coming unstuck during the fight, much discussion took place between the members of the Carp Catchers' Club to redress this problem. New ideas and theories that were thought up needed to be tried out, and what better way to start than at the beginning of a new season? This is what happened at the start of the 1954 season.

The hook-shedding problem affected not only Dick, for Maurice Ingham and Bob Richards had both hooked monster fish, only to have the hookhold give way after playing them for a while. Dick in particular had lost no fewer than four whoppers in this way during the previous two seasons. The discussion was mainly centred around the fact that many of the Redmire fishes' mouths were very much underslung. Pete Thomas pointed out that a hook struck upwards could scarcely help coming up against bone, into which it would penetrate only a little way, and that it would then come out again very easily. An idea was mooted to use a running lead stopped a few inches from the hook, thus making the hook penetrate the bottom lip. Used in conjunction with crust and an Arlesey bomb, Dick had already had success with this method at Dagenham in 1952.

Another problem at Redmire was that of finding a more appealing bait. This would take many more years to come to fruition, but all the while anglers fishing at the pool came to the conclusion that the carp's preoccupation not only with foods of a certain kind but also of a particular size meant that lumps of groundbait ought to be about the size of the hookbait.

Another absorbing problem concerned a big carp that fed along a sort of ledge at the dam at Redmire. This ledge was about 4ft wide and 5ft below the surface. Dick had hooked and lost this carp on the first visit back in 1952, and had noticed that the big carp would appear from one of the weedbeds at the eastern side of the dam and feed on groundbait along the ledge. If he or anyone else fished anywhere along the dam, no matter how quietly, the groundbait was left untouched, but if they went off and fished somewhere else, they found that the groundbait along the ledge was all eaten by morning! How could this problem be solved?

On 19 June 1954 Pete Thomas and Dick Walker arrived at Redmire. Again the weeds along each side of the lake were very thick and were all packed together with algae and scum. The only open water was a strip down the centre of the lake, 40–50yd wide and ending at the dam. The ledge was groundbaited and Dick fished until 4.30 a.m. Then he removed his baits and went to sleep. At that point the groundbait was untouched, but come the morning around 7 a.m. when he looked again it was all gone!

The next evening, Dick moved into the Willow pitch and cast diagonally to the right, so that the lead weight fell on the dam itself some 30–40yd away. The tackle consisted of one of Dick's carp rods – the double-built Mk III – a Mitchell reel, and 9lb breaking strain monofilament to which a carefully sharpened James size 3 hook was tied. A 1oz Arlesey bomb was stopped by a small shot about 6in from the hook. Dick walked round to the dam, found the tackle, baited with a piece of new flake the size of a man's fist, squeezed it tight so it would sink and dropped it neatly so it sank on to the ledge. Then he scattered about twenty similar pieces around it. Once back at the rod, he put it into the bite alarm (the new antenna type) and wound in the slack, even though the line was lying across a dense weedbed. Dick and Pete had a plan which would entail the use of the punt, and this was brought over and moored in a little bay just a

*Dick Walker's first design of the antenna bite alarm in 1954.*

*Dick Walker applies pressure to the weeded 34lb common. The rod in use is an early attempt at the ideal carp rod called the Mk III (now the property of the author).*

few yards away. That night they were joined by Bob Richards, and all three of them sat taking well past midnight. Bob then went and fished on the opposite bank, while Pete cast out to the left of where they were pitched. Nothing moved as the sun rose and its heat made the lake steam – a perfect morning. Then, close to 5 a.m., the bite alarm which had lain quiet all night suddenly burst into life and the line shot off through the rings at high speed. With Pete Thomas scrabbling for the camera, Dick picked up the rod, dropped in the pick-up and with a sweeping upward motion struck hard into whatever had picked up the bait. The rod arched over and the slipping clutch purred as the big carp moved fast up the centre of the lake. Then it turned and shot into some heavy

*The 34lb common safely on the bank. It proved to be Dick's second carp over 30lb – he was the first man to achieve this feat.*

*B.B.'s scraper-board drawing of the Redmire monster that was 'the size of a small rowing boat!'*

weed, within a matter of seconds coming to a halt. It was stuck fast, and not even fierce hand-lining could shift it an inch. By then, however, Pete had already unhitched the punt and had paddled it past the spot when Dick was standing. He jumped in – the chase was on.

Following the line across to where the fish was stuck proved not too difficult, even though scum and weeds had festooned themselves all along the line. Eventually, they came over the spot where the carp lay. Dick bent the rod more and more, and this had the desired effect as something moved way below. It began to move slowly at first, and then suddenly it came to the top and swirled heavily, sending water and weeds everywhere. With a mighty roll it set off out into open water. Pete Thomas paddled like fury as they

followed the carp up the lake, but by then Dick had the measure of the fish and, once in the clear, he meant it to stay there. After a dogged fight it eventually rolled again, this time straight into the bottom of the great triangle landing net. Dick dropped the rod, grabbed the net with both hands and heaved the carp into the punt.

There was the hook, right through its bottom lip! Slowly they paddled back, all the while Bob Richards standing on the dam taking photographs of the spectacle. He was on hand however, to help Pete lift the fish out of the punt and on to dry land. It was a big common carp, possibly the one that was the ledge feeder. It weighed a mighty 31lb 4oz, though here there is a tale to tell. When the weight was read the scales said 34lb exactly, but Dick shouted over to Bob Richards that it was the same weight as his old record – 31lb 4oz. Dick felt it prudent not to tell Bob that he had yet again taken a fish over Bob's record-breaking mirror of 1951.

**Monster on the Bank**

In early July Dick again went to Redmire, this time for what was a short two-day affair which turned out fishless as the carp yet again turned their noses up at his offerings. This wasn't surprising, for the carp were spawning for the second time that year. During the second day, however he was involved in witnessing and weighing the largest carp ever seen on the banks of an English water.

Dick had noticed that a female fish had been driven into shallow water by two or three smaller male fish. As this very large female carp had been driven so far into the shallow water close to the bank that it was lying on its side and looked in some danger of remaining permanently stranded, Dick paddled out to it. He clapped his big carp net over it, pulled it ashore, weighed it and then carried it down with some effort to the deep water near the dam and released it. But before the fish was placed back into Redmire he had carefully weighed the beast – all 58lb of it! This fish displayed a considerably distended body shape through spawn, so what it would have weighed in normal condition in late autumn Dick

*Dick Walker struggles to weigh the 'stranded mirror' – the scales read 58lb!*

would not have liked to guess. Apart from the considerably distended abdomen, it didn't actually look appreciably bigger than his record carp, but this fish does represent – even all these years later – the largest accurately weighed carp that has ever been recorded in the UK.

Unfortunately, Dick never took a picture of this fish – in fact, he kept the whole thing rather low key, saying, 'People were just getting used to my record 44lb carp as being quite genuine, let alone me telling them about capturing big carp at Redmire with a landing net!'

Maurice Ingham, that master carper from Lincolnshire was to figure in the Redmire catches of 1954 by capturing in August his second twenty-pounder. This fish also proved to be Redmire's first true leather carp, and it weighed 21lb 8oz, ending a long run of disasters that had struck over the previous few years. Maurice was a diligent carp angler and a real thinking man, one who covered every angle in the pursuit of carp. In contrast to other members of the Carp Catchers' Club, Maurice had built most of his own tackle – a carp rod and a circular-style landing net complete with a hand-made net. He was a great believer in groundbaiting for carp, and can rightfully claim to have made a considerable contribution to the catching of carp with potatoes and the correct application of feeding this bait. Funnily enough, when I met up with Maurice in 1991 he could remember but the briefest details of capturing this fish, telling me I knew more about the circumstances surrounding its capture than he did!

September came and with it Redmire was to greet three new anglers to its banks – a man-and-wife duo, Mr and Mrs Berth-Jones, and their friend Jack Opie. As all three arrived, so the Kefford brothers – Dick and Harry – were coming to the end of a week-long stint which had proved to be fruitless...so often the result when one fished Redmire.

Jack Opie was keen to start, and as soon as the Keffords had finished with their rods in the Willow pitch he set up his rod and cast out. Can you believe that within minutes of this, his buzzer sounded and the line poured off the spool? He struck and found himself firmly attached to a good-sized carp. A long battle ensued and all the while the Keffords looked on in stunned silence. When May Berth-Jones finally got the net under the big fish and the people present peered into the net, in the bottom lay a perfect fully-scaled

mirror which when weighed went to 27lb 5oz! The Keffords were lost for words and the Berth-Jones could not believe their luck in seeing a Redmire carp on the bank within minutes of arriving. Naturally, Jack Opie was in awe of the monster and after much thought asked Gerry if it were possible to have the fish set up. Gerry then spoke to Col. Maclean who gave his consent. This was a special 'Leney' carp, being of the fully-scaled mirror variety.

Look at the picture reproduced here. At a quick glance you might think it was a common carp because the mirror scales are uniformly quite small. Out of any batch of carp that Donald Leney hand-picked on his visits to Vaassen, this sort of carp was not often present. Jack Opie's fully-scaled mirror turned out to be an all-time Redmire best and lasted as a national full-scaled mirror record for many years.

Gerry and May Berth-Jones were so keen to fish the pool that they would have stopped there the whole summer if it was at all possible! Gerry told me years later, 'What a place it was, it was like looking into a vast aquarium, some of the fish seemed impossible...I know Dick [Walker] said there were carp present that could easily break his record, I knew that was true...for I saw them!'

If Jack Opie's catch seemed to be lucky, it was nothing compared to another friend of Dick Walker's who accompanied both Dick and Pete Thomas in October of that year. His name was Pat Russell. It was Pat who had helped with the setting up of Bob Richards' record fish back in 1951 by supplying the degreasing agent that Dick used in preserving the carcass. A complete novice, Pat was to turn the tables on both men on this trip, and right from the start he found both Pete's and Dick's behaviour somewhat unusual. After all, weren't the actions of a dedicated carp fisher all down to stealth and concealment? They arrived after dark, and he later said: 'Imagine my surprise when, once we parked the car, Dick and Pete went down to the lake and shone a large torch on the water.' Dick explained he would rather find out about the conditions in which he was going to fish at the start, then once this was

*Marvellous 27lb 5oz full-scaled mirror, captured by Jack Opie in September 1954 from the Willow pitch.*

*Pete Thomas prepares to net Pat Russell's 25lb leather. Note the log with two sticks jammed in position indicating drifting weed was a problem at the time.*

found out he would make as little noise as possible. When the lamp was turned on, it disturbed a big carp right in the margins, and that alone was enough to make Pat's mouth water.

After this episode Dick went to fish over by the twin balsams which mark Pitchford pitch, while Pete and Pat erected a small tent in the Willow pitch. All remained quiet until a strong breeze sprang up at first light. This disturbed the bite alarms, which were affected more by the floating scum than by the wind itself, but placing a small log in the water anchored by some sticks solved the problem. However, within half an hour the alarm sounded again, but this time the line could be seen to be running out quickly.

A successful strike by Pat made the rod buck in his hands as the fish set off on a strong run heading for the dam. Heavy sidestrain turned it, and soon it was close to the bank and turning over and over. Then it rolled on the surface, but this time into the waiting net held by Pete. He lifted the net by holding the mesh and got the whole lot on to the bank. Later this fine leather carp pulled the scales to 25lb. Besides the excitement of this capture – a new Redmire leather record – the other thing of note was that Dick Walker managed to record on film the entire events I have just outlined.

## Multiple Catch

Gerry Berth-Jones and his wife May found themselves in a unique position with the dawning of the new season of 1955 – they would be fishing for the first four days. Accompanying them would be a friend named Derrick Davenport, himself a notable fisherman.

Once at the lake the weed seemed not as bad as it had done in previous years. The men went off to see what fish they could find, and May was left to sort the camp out! Plenty of carp were in evidence and the men had seen some big fish too. They fished from the famed Willow pitch, but the first day produced no runs to any of the rods. Then conditions changed and with it so the carp came on the feed. The catch that followed was the first multiple bag of large carp the pool had ever produced.

First off the mark was Derrick with a 12lb common carp, although this fish became weeded and Gerry had to go in after it. When up to his waist in water, he finally netted the fish. His remarks on returning to the bank made his companions smile: 'I wouldn't have gone in if I'd known how heavy it wasn't!'

After this Derrick caught a real beauty of 22lb and Gerry landed a very pretty 18lb 4oz linear mirror. All three had watched the fight of this last fish in open water, and it was thrilling to see for the water was as clear as that from a tap. Until then, May's lines had never moved and she was beginning to think her chances of a Redmire carp were fading – certainly as far as this trip was concerned. But on the last day of their visit her buzzer at last signalled a run. Closing the pick-up and lifting the rod she struck firmly, standing up at the same time. The fish felt tremendous as it tore off for the centre of the pool. She held the rod high, dug the rubber button into her groin and held on for all she was worth. The carp became weeded, but in the meantime Derrick had fetched the punt. Without a moment's hesitation they jumped aboard and set course for the weeded fish. Once the strain came from above the carp moved, came to the surface and thrashed the water into a foam. May had dreamed of a fish like this many times but had also often wondered if, 'I would have the strength in my arms and wrists to beat it, now the test was on I found strength I never knew I possessed.'

Weed was all over the line and continually got stuck in the rod rings; it clung in great bunches and often made turning the reel impossible. While this was going on the carp suddenly decided to make for the shelter of the old boat house. With some considerable power it moved at speed for the obstacle, and May remembers the corks bending under her hand as she applied sidestrain. With a sinking heart she saw the carp make its goal, only to turn around abruptly and swim out again! The carp became more controllable and slowly they made their way back to the Willows. Once there, May and Derrick stepped ashore leaving Gerry to jump in and get ready to record the landing on film. The fish was safely netted and May's delight on seeing this carp on the bank had her grinning from ear to ear.

This indeed was a famous capture – Redmire had made May the first woman in carp-fishing history to land a twenty-pounder. The fine leather carp tipped the scales at 21lb 8oz. That carp was the fourth taken on that trip and made fishing headlines in the press of the day. Redmire, never for long out of the limelight, was again making the headlines!

*No wonder the big smile: May Berth-Jones becomes the first woman to land a carp over 20lb in England. A pure leather carp, it weighed 21lb 8oz.*

Would you believe after this promising start only one other big carp was caught that year – a 23lb common carp landed by Dick Walker in July? To add insult to injury, it turned out to be foulhooked in the left ventral fin. After this nothing more was heard of Redmire for nearly a year...

### Another Giant

Bob Richards was again to hit the headlines with another carp over 30lb. On Saturday, 21 July, while fishing at the pool with Allen Hind and Eddie Price, he had a strong run at 11 p.m. It took almost half an hour to subdue the fish and when it finally came to the bank it was found to be foulhooked.

Undoubtedly the carp had taken the baited hook, but somehow the hook had slipped and recaught under the chin of the fish – this explained why Bob had had so much trouble with it. It was put in a sack until morning, but inspection of the carp at first light revealed that it had died. The combination of a strong fight and a close-weave sack had unfortunately caused its death. It was, however a super-looking carp with measurements as follows: length 31¾in from nose to fork of tail; girth 27in. It weighed 31lb 8oz. It was taken away and set up by Eddie Price; and it lasts to this day. In fact, twenty years ago, when I first visited Eddie Price at his marvellous farm home in Gloucestershire, he managed to find this specimen in his loft! It had not seen the light of day for some years and immediately brought back the memory of its capture to Eddie. He later told me, 'Bob was a good angler who was more than a little dismayed at this big carp dying – it was his best fish ever.'

The weather in August of that year was good, and so was the fishing at Redmire!

Dick Walker and Pete Thomas took Pat Russell as a guest, and on 18 August Pat hit the jackpot. Fishing one rod in an area both Dick and Pete thought was poor, he caught three carp between noon and 4 p.m.: a small one, plus an 18lb 8oz and a 27lb mirror! Both of the latter were superb-looking Leney 'linear' mirrors. An interesting point, and one that was noticed by the anglers, was that both of these carp were the same length, although there was nearly 10lb difference in weight. As Dick Walker pointed out, it showed just how hard it was to judge accurately the weight of some fish when viewed in the water. Another excellent set of photographs was taken by Dick of the whole fight, including dramatic shots of the netting which featured Pete Thomas and Pat. This photographic work, mainly by Dick while he was carp fishing, was another important factor in the acceptance by anglers that carp was the species to go with. Photography was nothing new to Dick: he had become proficient in the art long before he started fishing at Redmire. His evocative work with the camera captured for all to see the excitement that catching big carp was all about.

Before August was out two other carp anglers were to realize their Redmire dreams by catching carp over 20lb.

Dick Kingsley-Kefford's brother Harry, who had fished as a guest of Carp Catchers' Club member Jack Smith, finally came into contact with a big carp. Fishing in his favourite spot – the

*Bob Rutland appears from under a camouflaged 'bell' tent in the Willow pitch; in the background the mighty willow is in evidence.*

10

Willow pitch – he connected with a common carp during the early evening. It was soon landed and turned out to be a quite fat 25-pounder. After a night in a sack, however, this fish also died, the close weave of the sack again being to blame. It was taken back to Norfolk and set up by Harry's brother Dick. Harry's fishing partner, Jack Smith, the Bradford-upon-Avon carpman, also saw his line race away during the same session. This fish was landed from the Willow pitch and weighed 22lb, but unfortunately was foulhooked in the flank. The photograph that you see is the only one that was taken, and I was very lucky indeed to find it after much detective work sifting through many letters from over twenty years ago!

One further big carp was caught during the 1956 season, making it the most successful year for big fish (five in total) at Redmire.

This last fish was indeed most deserved for the angler concerned. Throughout the years he had seen his fishing companions catch 20lb carp from Redmire, but now his turn had come. Caught in dramatic circumstances (which included taking to the punt), Gerry Berth-Jones at last landed a super 21lb 8oz common carp. Success through hard work had paid dividends, and the run had come from the famed Pitchford's Pit – the place where the deep hole was!

After the success of 1956, by contrast the two following years produced nothing of any great note. Why this happened is hard to say. The methods and baits in use were more or less the same as from the first years, and most areas in the lake were tried at one stage or another. Perhaps the stalking aspect might have been tried more, or a more liberal use of different baits might have paved the way to greater success. In any event, the carp were beginning to win the fight, so to speak. To put this into perspective, the pressure the water received is nothing like that of today – most of the fishermen who fished at Redmire through the 1950s only managed maybe two or three good weekend sessions. Even Bob Richards who was a local didn't go as much as he would have liked. In reality, members of the Carp Catchers' Club were keen not to abuse the kind offer that Col. Maclean had extended to them.

## MONSTERS ARE SPOTTED

Although Redmire was to prove difficult in the extreme during the 1957/58 season, the pool was still fished extensively by all the Carp Catchers' Club members. Come the start of the 1958 season and several fish were yet again lost. Gerry Berth-Jones hooked a big carp one morning from Pitchford's Pit, but this fish got stuck in the weed and even going out in the punt couldn't save a disaster, and Maurice Ingham also had a tussle with a giant in the same pitch, but again nothing came of it. However, a tremendously important event took place in July 1958.

Eddie Price, a Gloucestershire angler and close friend of Bob Richards, had fished as a guest of Bob on and off for a couple of years. He had hooked at least one very good carp during these trips, but as another visit was arranged around the middle of July 1958 he could never have dreamed what a spectacle would confront him during these three days at Redmire.

The weed was as bad as ever and the weather was quite warm. During Sunday at around mid-day Eddie decided he'd take the punt out and drift quietly down the length of the pool. These boating trips which most, if not all, the people who fished the lake tried at one time or the other, were fascinating. Often they were treated to a view of a big carp gliding past as the punt drifted the length of the pool. This day Eddie pushed off from the dam and drifted quietly past the Willow pitch some 20yd from the shore. The water was gin-clear and Eddie remembers being able to see the bottom through 8ft of water. After twenty minutes or so he arrived a little further down the lake and came to some shallow water adjacent to the Stile pitch. Looking over towards an extensive weedbed he spied a dark shape which was obviously a carp lying quite close to the surface. Slowly the punt moved closer to the basking carp. Eddie looked closer and then realized that the only part of the fish visible was the head and shoulders, but mind you, these alone looked big.

Then he was close – perhaps 8–10 ft away. He slowly stood up, shielding his eyes. This carp couldn't be real – indeed, the head and back of

*Perhaps the most important picture ever taken at Redmire. Eddie Price's leviathan…it might have weighed 60–70lb!*

the carp were in a clear patch in the weed and the sight of these made Eddie catch his breath…it was a leviathan! Then, in a stroke of genius, he gently moved away, without so much as a ripple and made for the bank.

Once ashore he dived for his tackle bag, for in the bottom lay a camera. Once this was found he went back to the punt. Could he manage to record the monster on photographic film? He could only hope that the carp had stayed in the same spot and not vanished into the depths, never to been seen again.

Lady Luck was on Eddie's side that morning, for when he came back to the same spot there lay the carp – it had hardly moved. Then, within a yard of the beast, he raised the camera and took a picture. He took another frame, but the fish had at last sensed the closeness of the punt and its sailor, and it moved forward out into the clear water. Eddie's eyes followed it; this had to be the king of all carp. He raised the camera again and took another picture, but then, as Eddie's eyes almost popped out of his head, the fish serenely went directly under the punt. Could this be true – at one point Eddie saw the head and tail on either side of the punt, the width of which is around 3ft! In a few seconds it was gone with a gentle flick of its tail, and with it a memory that

lasts to this day. At the time Eddie thought he'd seen a 50lb plus carp, but with the benefit of landing a forty-pounder himself the following year, he soon realized that the fish he had seen that day was far, far larger…

The three pictures that Eddie Price took that day have been studied by myself – indeed, these pictures might never have come to light had it not been for the correspondence that took place between the two of us. Eddie wrote in May 1970: 'I have a negative of a photo I am very proud of – a carp of over 70lb lying in the weeds at Redmire, TRUTH!!' I wrote back, 'Please send it, quick!' This Eddie did, and the prints that I had developed showed a carp that was extraordinary. The first frame (which is reproduced here) and the second were almost identical, and the third (the one which showed the complete fish) was unfortunately spoiled by the dazzle off the water's surface. Even with modern-day photographic techniques little can be seen on the film. However, the first picture in the sequence is the one that has become famous. Twenty years ago I showed it to Dick Walker, Pete Thomas, Gerry Berth-Jones, Maurice Ingham and the like. All said that there was little in the picture by which to gauge the size of the carp, but the general opinion was that this was a picture of perhaps, a

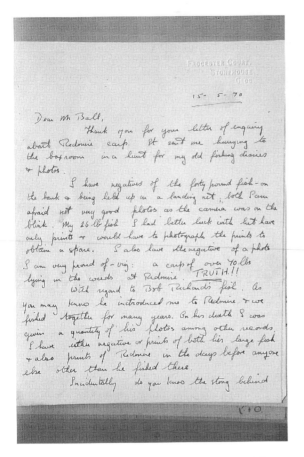

*Original letter to the author stating the existence of the 'monster' photograph.*

Redmire carp the likes of which all the anglers mentioned had seen at some stage or other. The size? All agreed with Eddie Price that it was in the 60–70lb range. This one picture is all we have as some kind of photographic evidence to the existence of a super-sized Redmire 'Leney' carp.

### Another Forty-Pounder!

In July 1959 a long-time friend of Dick Walker and Pete Thomas made a visit to Redmire as a guest of these two. It was only Bob Rutland's third trip to the carp angler's Mecca and this time he hit the jackpot. Fishing from the Willow pitch, he had a run one morning that resulted in a long tussle of which the outcome was uncertain for some while. But success came as the carp was eventually landed. It turned out to be a beautiful linear carp weighing exactly 25lb. However, it was found to be foulhooked in the tail, so no wonder Bob had had such a battle with it. July gave way to a hot August and the carp refused to feed despite anglers' baits being placed in all the likely spots. It was to be the end of September before Redmire would startle the angling world again with another mighty mirror carp.

This time it would be Eddie Price's turn to bring Redmire into the headlines. As with many stories in fishing it was full of drama. For a start he very nearly didn't go at all, but knowing that Bob Richards and Allan Hind had a visit arranged and the thought of the monster he'd seen the year before was too much for Eddie. Arriving soon after daybreak on the 27th conditions seemed perfect – it had been settled and warm for several days. The weed that had been so thick earlier in the season had almost gone, but the water's colour indicated that the fish were feeding; in fact, bubbling could be seen almost everywhere.

Although Eddie baited up for the three of them, he actually fished in the undisturbed shallows. Up until 10 a.m. the weather had been the same as when he had arrived, but then a dramatic change took place. A chilly easterly wind swept down the lake, the heat vanished and with it the pool went completely dead. Bob and Allan arrived about this time, and all three men thought that they were in for a cold night. Eddie decided to fish the Stile pitch while the other two chose spots up by the willows.

It did indeed turn out to be a very cold night, and when Eddie awoke everything was covered in a hoar frost and the lake steamed in a thick mist! At 5.30 a.m. Bob Richards came down the bank – both he and Allan had spent an uncomfortable night just sitting in deckchairs with blankets around them. By contrast, Eddie had buried himself deep inside a sheepskin flying suit, bedroll and tarpaulin. With the chance of a fish being somewhat slim, Eddie then left his tackle for a few minutes to get a fresh cup of tea and some breakfast back up where Bob and Allan were sitting.

*Eddie Price holds Redmire's second forty-pounder. Catching this carp convinced him that the fish he had seen (and photographed) the year before was far larger!*

Eddie had two sets of tackle out: both were B. James & Sons Dick Walker rods, one being a Mk IV carp, the other being a lighter Avon model. Both were baited with paste bait. The Mk IV was cast to the edge of the deeper water, about 30yd out, while the Avon was cast close to the edge just to the right of the swim. The buzzer suddenly sounded on the Avon rod and the line slowly peeled off the open spool. A quick strike brought a heavy lunge, the rod doubled over and the reel's clutch shrieked with the pull of the fish. Bob and Allan heard the commotion and were soon by Eddie's side. The carp kept close to the bank for a couple of minutes but then, seemingly bored with the whole proceedings, set off on a long run straight out. However, Eddie was a skilful angler and his patience paid off. As the fish came close he pushed the net out directly in front of where the fish swam. He made no mistake and the carp plunged straight into the bottom of the net's folds. It was a veritable monster that he and his companions looked down on in the wet grass. The pointer of the big scales registered exactly halfway between 40lb and 41lb – 40lb 8oz, and was the second largest carp ever landed. This particular carp was to have a famous life from that point on, but more of this later.

## A New Decade

The start of the 1960s saw carp fishing gaining in popularity throughout the length of the country. At Redmire it also meant that its occupants had been fished for nearly ten years. Nowhere in the country had there come a carp anywhere near the size of the Redmire fish, so what else had Redmire in store for its anglers?

When Pat Russell and Pete Thomas went in June 1960 both caught good carp. Surprisingly these fish were caught on the same day. Pat Russell had managed to subdue a 27lb leather which was foulhooked in the tail, whilst Pete Thomas captured a super 20lb common carp. Their companion Bob Rutland, who had found success the year before, also hooked a big carp but this fish slipped the hook after a long tussle.

Dick Walker visited the pool during the summer as did Bob Richards, but the carp steadfastly refused all offerings and it was not until September that another carp came to the bank. It was to be Eddie Price who captured this leather carp of 26lb. He was back in his favourite swim, the Stile pitch. After spending a lone vigil through the night, at 8 a.m., his bite alarm burst into action as a steady run came to a bait cast out into the deeper water. Making no mistakes, Eddie landed the fish in short order and Bob Richards was on hand to take the photographs.

The angling pressure at Redmire was beginning to decrease in this period. Dick Walker, always an all-rounder, was just as happy catching huge roach or big barbel. B. B., Maurice Ingham and Gerry Berth-Jones all paid but a few visits to the pool, and local angler Bob Richards went fishing less due to deteriorating health. Though carp fishers might not have shown so much interest in the pool, the fish of dreams were still there to be caught. Many of the carp were coming up to their thirtieth year, and in among these were the monsters. Although none as far as I am aware had been seen since Eddie Price's historic picture in 1958, the plain fact remained that they still languished in Redmire's depths. However, it would be some years before anglers came close to them again.

*Rare early picture of two Redmire carp on the bank together, captured by Pat Russell (not in photo), 27lb, and Pete Thomas, 20lb. This photograph, taken in June 1960, was towards the end of the Carp Catchers' Club reign at Redmire.*

In the meantime, Redmire was still being fished. In 1961 John Nixon, who as a guest of Dick Kingsley-Kefford fished the pool for the first week of the season, accounted for a super 23lb carp. John was a 'Walker' style of angler and had been successful in the carp-catching stakes in the 1950s. I believe this visit was one of John's first and to catch a fish like this was quite a surprise. This fish, a leather carp, was nicknamed Raspberry because of the huge bowl of that fruit that was presented by Col. Maclean to both Dick Kefford and John, prior to John connecting with the carp. Later, when this fish figured in the Jack Hilton 'syndicate' period, it displayed small red

*John Nixon with Raspberry at 23lb – note the tie!*

spots along the lower half of its flank and Jack assumed that this was the reason the name had been given. He was unaware of the raspberry feast incident.

Raspberry turned out to be the only 20lb carp caught at the pool that year and reflected the poor results that persisted throughout this period of Redmire's history. Had the carp learned quicker than the anglers? Or was it just that the pool did not get fished that often? Probably it was a combination of both that made Redmire figure little in the headlines of the day. That said, at times Redmire could not fail to make the news, and in 1962 it was given a centre-spread feature in *Angling Times*. It was a special photo feature by Dick Walker that led to this article, but it wasn't Dick who caught the fish.

That first week of the season Walker had visited the pool with the Taylor Brothers. They arrived to find the pool heavily weeded and almost unfishable, except from the dam where the water is deepest. Because of the warm weather most of the carp were rolling in the water at the opposite end of the lake where the water is shallow, but Joe noticed a fish swimming up and down at the edge of the weeds at the dam end, and decided to try a floating crust bait. The fish, after inspecting this and turning away several times, was finally hooked. It bolted through the weeds and emerged in a narrow strip of open water between the weedbed and the bank, where it became stuck. Joe Taylor, the angler who had hooked the fish, was stuck on one side of the weedbed with the fish on the other, and neither was able to do much about it. However, Fred J. Taylor solved the problem by wading out with a long-handled net. The first step took him in up to his knees, and the second to his waist. He looked round and said plaintively, 'That's funny, the water only came two inches up them ducks!'

*'Funny, it only came 2in up them ducks!' Fred J. Taylor wades out for his brother Joe's 26lb leather carp caught in June 1960.*

It took Fred a fair amount of poking about in the weeds to move the fish, but it came to the surface at last and was finally netted. It weighed 26lb and was Joe's personal best and a fine fish with which to start the season. This example of superb photographic evidence to back a good story by Dick Walker made another big impression on the British angling public. Dick's photographic work was special during the 1950s and there can be little doubt that this, along with the actual carp catches made the sport of carp fishing much more acceptable to the ordinary angler.

The capture of Joe Taylor's carp so early in the season looked like making it a vintage year for Redmire, but as we have seen in years gone by the Redmire carp weren't remotely impressed – in fact, they were so remarkably unimpressed that not one took a baited hook for the rest of the season!

## The End...Nearly!

Something was to happen to Redmire and the British Isles that changed the face of fisheries right across the country – the incredible winter of 1962/63. It locked most of the UK's stillwaters and some of the rivers (including the Thames) in ice that was to last for over three months. At Redmire they drove a tractor across the pool and a herd of cattle wandered out on to its icy expanse. The effect this cold blast had on the fish stocks of this country was enormous – a massive fish kill followed the melting of the icy water and a great fear for the Redmire carp was expressed by many people. I believe some corpses were found once the ice had melted, although whether this actually happened is unclear. In the spring, British anglers buried the dead – in their thousands. Even carp, one of the hardiest of all coarse fish, had succumbed in many waters.

*John Nixon looking for signs of carp in the spring of 1963, only a few months after the ice which had locked Redmire solid for over six weeks.*

During the spring of 1963 John Nixon spent a day at the pool looking for any sign of a disaster as he had heard of some corpses being found. That day, spent drifting around in the punt, proved fruitless with hardly a fish being seen. Was it true then – could it be that the Redmire carp had succumbed just like countless other carp had done? On the face of it, it did seem that this was the case.

Then in September 1963 Pete Thomas caught a glorious 20lb common carp. Fred J. Taylor was on hand to help Pete. It was only the second carp Fred had seen on the banks of Redmire in many years of visiting the water. Fred himself had not had a single chance of a fish during all this time, but such is fishing! Pete Thomas's carp gave hope to the Carp Catchers' Club that maybe some carp after all had survived the icy ordeal. However, members visited it less and less during the next two years and no reports of big carp were heard of. By March 1965 *Angling Times* ran the headline, 'No More Records', stating that the Carp Catchers' Club thought only a few small to medium carp existed in Redmire Pool at that time. However, it is at this point that the Redmire story takes a twist, for by the mid-1960s a new breed of angler was starting to make a name for itself. The specimen hunter!

This movement had started some years before, and it has to be said that it was Dick Walker and the Carp Catchers' Club that provided the catalyst for the evolution of the specimen hunter. By the mid-1960s there were many such specimen hunting groups around in England. One of the first was the Kent Specimen Group; their membership was less than ten, but all were keen young men with good catches of specimen fish – especially carp. Carp was to be the original cult fish.

Two members of the Kent Specimen Group namely Grahame Igglesden and Bob Rolph, decided to find the famous Redmire Pool for themselves. It was at the end of March 1965, and with the weather being quite mild they took an Ordnance Survey map and boldly went where no specimen hunter had been before! Cleverly walking across the fields higher up the valley so as not to raise the alarm with the farmer or his workhands, they found themselves at the Redmire shallows.

'It was so small,' Grahame recalled when we met recently, adding, 'We walked round for maybe a couple of hours, the water was clear and almost straight away we saw some carp. Then we saw one or two which looked to be over 20lb. All told, we saw plenty of carp and were then puzzled by the reports of the fish dying. It seemed to us that the lake was full of carp, with some big ones as well.'

Arriving home these two men told of their experience to others; Grahame Igglesden had written for *The Creel* angling magazine and knew the editor, John Nixon, quite well. Knowing John's association with the pool, Grahame told John Nixon of his trip and what he'd seen. He said, 'John was more than a little surprised to hear this news, and was keen to know of what carp we had seen. I think he'd hatched a plan to organize some fishing soon after I put the phone down!'

So Redmire was to come alive again through Grahame Igglesden and Bob Rolph initially, but later it was John Nixon's tenacity in negotiating with a firm of solicitors in London who were acting on behalf of the owners that led to him clinching the deal. Other things changed at this time: Col. Maclean left the estate and so ended the Carp Catchers' Club's exclusive privilege to fish

Redmire. On the face of it this might seem something of a disappointment, but in truth the fishing by members of the club had virtually ceased between 1963 and 1965. The common-held belief was that many of the big fish had died and interest from then on had gradually ebbed away.

That fact couldn't have been further from the truth, however, and the Redmire carp – at least, the originals – were only middle-aged by then, being in their thirty-third year. True enough the big freeze-up of 1962/3 had claimed lives and other odd fish had died through the years, but that said, it could be guessed that at least thirty carp from the original 1933 batch were alive in 1965. Not forgetting the other generations of carp that followed, some of which were well into the 20lb range or more at that time. How do we know this? Well, as Redmire became well fished

again large common carp began to dominate the catches, and almost every one of these would have been a spawned fish. We've already seen how this kind of carp was far more hardy in its make-up so could have survived that bitter winter, and reports from anglers indicated that small mirror and leather carp were rarely seen and even more rarely captured. So, thirty-odd years on from the time of stocking the numbers of carp the pool held were considerable and most of these were big fish. The ability of Redmire to support this kind of poundage was extraordinary, and it was still a very special water.

**A New Regime**
The season of 1966/7 marked yet another chapter in Redmire's history, as members of the major specimen groups were given the chance to fish

*Unique picture of Redmire taken from a tree above the shallows in the days when John Nixon controlled the fishing.*

the pool on day tickets under the scheme John Nixon had set up. From this time on Redmire was to receive a barrage of angling pressure from a new generation of resolute carp fishers. Even with new methods, better tackle and different baits Redmire carp proved as difficult as ever. However, it cannot be denied that some wonderful carp were landed, including the third largest carp ever caught. This carp, caught by Roger Bowskill of the Devon Specimen Group in September, weighed 38lb 8oz. It turned out to be the same carp as Eddie Price's monster of seven years previously. This carp also has the notorious claim of being the only one to leave Redmire and the Bernithan Estate completely…and yet return. Let me explain.

After this fish was landed the size of it appeared to be too much for any of the scales available. So after some thought Roger and his colleagues decided to wrap the fish in a very wet sack and transport it to Llangarron. Once there, a local store with suitable scales was found and the fish's weight was accurately verified. What a spectacle this was – housewives and shop owners came out to see this monster live fish being carefully manhandled in their local high street! A short time later the big carp was safely swimming back at Redmire, appearing none the worse for its

experience. Subsequently, some fifteen years later this carp became Chris Yates' new record of 51lb 8oz!

The following year of 1967 turned out to be Roger Bowskill's year as well. He landed another monster carp over 30lb as well as a glorious 24lb common. That year also saw Brian Hook of the Essex Specimen Group land a trio of carp all over 20lb in the space of some twenty-four hours! These were caught on the then new carp wonder bait – sausage paste. These two summers of fishing by the specimen groups proved that the Redmire carp were still very much alive and, more to the point, so were the monsters. During this time several carp were spotted by these experienced anglers that far outshone anything that had been landed. The magical monsters were still out there, hidden within the depths – could the re-awakening of Redmire's fishing by these younger anglers put one on the bank? Much talk ensued.

Towards the end of the summer of 1967 a party of four angling friends made the pilgrimage to Redmire. They were to spend a total of eight days at the pool, days that were filled with rainy weather. Huddled beneath their brollies, Grahame Igglesden, Mike Mintram and Roger Smith sat and watched lifeless lines, but the

*This picture taken by Chris Yates (in his first year at Redmire in 1972) clearly shows the punt in a state of disrepair, and also the once-famous willow tree – which came down in a storm one night – lying dead.*

fourth member of the party was to land a fish that sparked such fire and emotion within his soul that Redmire was to dominate his life for the next eight years. His name was Jack Hilton.

Jack's fish was a superb 35lb 'Leney' linear mirror and turned out to be the heaviest recorded carp of the season. In between the heavy rain-storms Jack had also spied more than one carp that was far larger than this fish. From that day on Redmire and its carp had Jack Hilton by the throat; he couldn't wait to return – but that was not to be until the following year.

During the early part of the close season of 1968 he phoned John Nixon with the intention of booking some dates during the coming season. He was shocked to be told by John that the fishing agreement with Redmire's executors was not to continue. The reason put forward was that litter left by a few unthoughtful people, along with their general bad behaviour, had put the fishing in jeopardy.

The subsequent events that transpired when Jack Hilton decided to do something about this situation is outside the scope of this chapter, but is extensively covered in Jack's own excellent book, *Quest for Carp*. I recommend you either purchase a copy second-hand, or go to your local library. I can also recommend *Redmire Pool* by Len Arbery and Kevin Clifford (Pelham Books, 1972) as the definitive work on the 1970s and 1980s at the pool.

Needless to say, Redmire's historic 'Leney' carp were far from finished in terms of astounding the angling world – indeed, the legend of the water was to grow in status as the years went by.

## THE 1990s

Let me now catapult you forward in time to the 1990s, for Redmire is still very much part of the current carp scene. Incredibly, so are some of the original carp! Below is an account of how I met some of Redmire's elderly citizens in somewhat unusual circumstances!

I'm still excited as I write this, for just a few days have passed since I visited the carp angler's Mecca: the magical Redmire Pool. Nothing strange in that, but this trip was to be special and a total one-off. For that day Redmire was to be netted...How did this come to happen and why was it even contemplated? In reality, this story has its roots several years ago at Redmire, for during this time the pool had become overrun with small carp. The main reason this had come to pass was because of the more recent comparatively mild winters. During the last three years the fingerlings from successful spawning of the Redmire carp have had a much greater survival through their important first winter. This may have been coupled with a decline in the eel population that would otherwise have hoovered up great amounts of spawn. But whatever the reason, if you were fishing at Redmire at the time you have had to have been a blind man not to notice that the pool was overstocked.

People who have fished at Redmire since the Carp Society took control (mainly through Les Bamford's endeavours) have gone there because it is legendary. Everyone's aim is to try to catch one of the pool's magnificent fish, mainly the large common carp. At a guess, I don't think people at the time were too bothered about catching just 4–5lb fish – being at Redmire was enough, and catching anything was a bonus! But these small fish were beginning to dominate the fishing, reducing the likelihood of a better carp getting to the bait first.

So the decision was taken to thin out these small carp. Les Bamford had thought long and hard on how this could be administered and by careful planning an idea came together. The first thought, however, was to fish for them and remove them as and when they were caught but it was deemed that this would take too long – maybe a season or two. Another idea was to lay trap-nets at various points around the pool to catch these small fish, but this too was rejected as the fish might come to some harm.

This left Les with the option of bringing in a professional fisheries company to net the water. After this, another important decision was taken: namely to lower the water level, for this would help greatly once a large net was hauled through

*Redmire these days, still a beautiful water.*

Redmire. As can be imagined, a great deal of thought, effort and sheer hard work came together to make it all happen. First, water pumps had to be installed and their progress carefully monitored – the water was taken away over the dam and then down into the stream, finally ending at Little Redmire, a fairly small pond further down the valley. Major earthworks constructed by Les and the Carp Society have made this an ideal holding pond for fish. So the plan was hatched and the date was set.

This is when I had a stroke of luck. One day I had to talk to Les Bamford on another matter, and at the end of the conversation he casually mentioned the netting affair. I stuttered slightly, saying to Les, 'Would it be possible for me to come along and witness this unique event?' I added, 'I'd love to *touch* one of those old boys, that's all.'

I could hear Les giggling on the other end of the phone, 'You're mad Chris Ball, mad as a snake,' he said, trying to stop laughing. 'Course you can come,' he added. That was it, I now had a chance that was second to none. 'Thanks Les,

see you at the pool on Sunday,' I retorted in a slightly intoxicated tone.

Setting off early on Sunday morning and driving along almost empty roads was a pleasure, and I completed the journey in just over two hours. Coasting down the hill at Redmire I pulled up amongst a group of cars – some of these belonged to tireless chaps who had been hard at it for most of the weekend. Once parked it was straight over to the Redmire hut. People were milling round, and in the thick of them was Les Bamford. 'About time Chris, the net's already out – have you ever seen Redmire like this?' Les said, pointing over towards the dam.

'Good grief,' I thought to myself, 'Where's the water?' For Redmire looked like a small puddle. At a guess, it had shrunk to two-thirds its size. The shallows were completely exposed, for the water didn't start until after the Redmire islands, and when I looked over the dam rail the water was some 5–6ft below me. The gently sloping sides of the lake were evident as I looked both left and right up the pool from where I stood. (As an aside here, in recent weeks I've talked and shown pictures to one of the long-time Redmire syndicate members. He thought the water level that day was as low as during the terrible dry summer that Redmire endured in 1976.)

Back to the netting, looking out from the dam I could see a huge net stretched across Redmire, and already there were teams of netsmen hauling at both ends. They struggled through the silt and mud, but were well prepared – several had wetsuits on – and a boat was on hand. It was to take some time before the net would close and the contents examined, but already the site at which to bring the net ashore was fixed. This was to be at the new boat house situated by the corner of the dam and just to the right of the famous Willow pitch.

By then most people had gathered at this point, and there at the ready were big tubs to hold the anticipated transfer of carp. One end of the net swept along the dam wall while men brought the by then heavy net tight along the margins from the left. Looking out at the huge circle of the net, every now and then a fish swirled over the top, and at one stage I saw clearly a big fish porpoise over! This shows how difficult carp are to net, and I've seen it happen before. However, soon the net became tighter, and with netmen behind its end and the bottom drawn up, now was the time to see what we had!

Quite frankly it took your breath away, for when there was only just a couple of feet of water the carp were revealed. Huge backs were visible as water was sprayed everywhere. Now was the time to work quickly, for it was evident that the net had caught some of Redmire's small carp. At a guess there might have been thirty or forty removed. I examined several – they displayed a most startling attribute for 'Leney' fish, for nearly all had high, almost vertical backs and were incredibly deep. These smallish carp were many generations removed from the original stocking of fifty carp in 1934. At the time those fish were two-year-olds, so the original stock fish were spawned at the fish farm in Holland in the early summer of 1932.

Several of Redmire's long-standing syndicate members have since told me that when these

*The author with Raspberry, one of Redmire's most famous residents.*

small fish reach double figures the 'humped' shoulders and great depth becomes smoothed out. Strange that? But if you think that's weird, wait until I tell you that of the 150 carp that were removed from Redmire during this netting operation; each of those carp except *one* was of the common carp scaling. Yes, just one single mirror carp was captured.

The reason for this is again fascinating. You might already know this but the common carp is the main base species of *Cyprinus carpio*. The other varieties of carp such as the mirror, leather and fully-scaled mirrors are all mutations from the original. These fish, unlike the commons (in Redmire at least), are not hardy enough to last that all-important first winter. When we look at the fabulous big old mirrors that have dominated the large fish captures at Redmire for over forty years, almost every one of these carp is from the original stocking. But there is hope . . .

Two years ago, after the carp had spawned, Les Bamford instructed that a quantity of small fry should be netted out. In amongst these wonderful tiny fish were the mirror, linear and fully-scaled types. They were transferred and reared on in specially constructed tanks that were housed in the big barn at Redmire. They survived, and a year later, when the fish were just palm-sized, they were removed and put into the lower lake. I'm glad to report that they've now been transferred back into Redmire itself. This is a brilliant idea to self-perpetuate Redmire with the superb mirror-type strain. Several of these little carp are stunning fully-scaled mirrors – I wonder, will these carp grow into the monsters of the future? At a guess, I think they might.

Anyway, I digress, so back to the action. When the net was lifted clear many beautiful carp were evident. I lost count of the big common carp that were slipped back into Redmire. I also glimpsed a couple of the big old mirrors as they were carefully lifted over the net. What a sight...!

Once this first sweep of the net was complete and the small carp had been removed it was time for a break. Back to the hut we all went, then it was breakfast time with John and Eileen Walker cooking a feast for the men. While we were all standing around Les Bamford suddenly darted off, only to return with both hands hidden behind his back. 'Guess what I've got here Chris?' he beamed. 'Don't know Les, surprise me!' I said. With that, out in the open came a pot and a pan. Both were black with age. 'What are those?' I asked. Looking serious, Les carefully explained. 'What with the water being so low, we've dragged these out of Redmire. I reckon this one belonged to Dick Walker and the other to Yatesy.'

Now don't laugh, for I looked at them and one indeed looked ancient. It was an old-styled saucepan that could have been used by someone to boil potatoes...maybe Dick Walker himself!

'Any chance of a memento?' I asked. 'Can't do that,' said Les, adding, 'I'll put them up for auction at the Carp Society Conference.' Several other people nodded in agreement.

Shortly after it was back to work as the netting team started the long, slow job of laying the net up in the Redmire shallows. Meanwhile, I managed to walk around the lake at this stage, but had got no further than the Style pitch on the western bank when the boss of the netting company shouted over to me. 'Come and have a look, Chris,' he said, pointing to a shape just out from the bank. I went to investigate, and to my surprise 5–8yd from the bank was a circular depression in the lake bed, then some distance away was another. Without doubt, these were the areas

where the fish had been feeding prior to the water being pumped out (the water had disappeared quickly). Many Redmire anglers in the past have reported fish standing on their heads up to their gills in the silt while searching out food. I spotted a few of these holes about the pool. They are the hotspots – for a small fee I could tell you where...only joking!

Later the netsmen were almost finished again, and this time Les Bamford wanted a closer count of the big fish and, if possible, the whoppers quickly weighed. Believe me, if you get a chance to fish Redmire then take it, for there were fish to over 30lb in the net!

Now was my moment as Les said, 'Let him in the water, the romantic old sod!'

The mud and silt made my progress out from the bank difficult, but soon there I was in the middle of the net. There were 20lb commons bumping into my legs as I was lost in a sea of Redmire carp!

That was quite something, I can tell you. Just to one side of me I spotted the unmistakable scaling of a Redmire linear mirror. What a beauty! I slipped a weigh-sling under it – at 21lb it was a totally immaculate, unmarked fish and I carefully held it as the cameras clicked away. But the best was yet to come. 'Here's one for you,' said a helper, pointing to a big carp in the water. Straight away I recognized this famous carp – it was the one I had come for.

My fingers lightly touched the almost bare flanks, and we looked closely into one another's eyes. Incredible as it sounds, here was a carp that could give me ten years or more in age, for it was Raspberry, a fish that is fifty-nine years old! Raspberry was a credit to all the carp anglers who have ever banked this much-loved carp – it was first captured by John Nixon back in June 1961 – for its condition was first class. I looked into the mouth – it seemed fine and the general appearance would never indicate the fish's age.

With great reverence I held and kissed this fish, much to the amusement of the crowd, before slipping it back over the net. Then all went quiet...I then heard someone say...'You're mad Chris Ball, mad as a snake.'

# 3 FRENSHAM PONDS – LOCAL TO LENEY

*This extraordinary lake which is situated in Surrey held my, and many other carp fishers' attention during the early 1980s, with the most beautiful big carp I have ever seen...or caught!*

## EARLY YEARS

Amidst the rolling countryside of deepest Surrey and set in an area of lush heather and gorse, tall pines and sandy ground, there sit two ponds of outstanding beauty and note. These depression-like features in the landscape have been filled with water for centuries. The Big Pond is some 60 acres in size, the Little Pond is almost 30 acres, and together they are called Frensham Ponds.

It's now almost ten years since this area of Surrey first became a part of my carp fishing days – almost to the exclusion of all other lakes. For three years it dominated my life so much that never before or since has the 'fever' been so strong within me, such was the fire that Frensham evoked within my soul.

This story of Frensham and its Leney carp is complete, for I'll tell of its beginning, middle and ending.

The beginning stretches back to at least the 17th century and probably before. Reference to these stretches of water can be found in a number of country books covering this part of the world. One was written by John Aubrey, the noted antiquary, who 'perambulated' Surrey in 1673 and 1674. He gives information on Frensham and its fish as follows: 'well known for its carps to the London fishmongers'. Another delightful volume from the early part of the 20th century called *Highways and Byways in Surrey*

*Idyllic surroundings – a 30lb mirror swirls near the net.*

retraces walks around this part of West Surrey. Its author described his first view of the ponds as follows:

'The grassy path runs on, until on a sudden bend the ground rises, and over a wooden stile opens out the vista of the great "Frensham Pond". The pond has often been painted, but this is the view I should choose, as I saw it first. To one coming up from these green depths of pasture, the air blows across the water with the freshness of the sea.'

As can be seen, Frensham's association with carp goes back for centuries. However, these 'carps to the London fishmongers' were almost certainly what we would term today as wild carp, for although it seems they were present in reasonable quantities at that time, come the turn of the present century few remained. References to the fish stocks at that time (1902), give note to pike, perch and tench, but not to carp.

One thing we can be sure of is that no fish lived in these ponds through World War II, for both were completely drained. Security reasons were behind this move, for to the north of Frensham lay the home of the British Army, Aldershot – not to mention the famous Farnborough Aerodrome, the aeronautical research centre where amongst other 'secret' activities afoot was the advanced development of radar. Here we have a connection with Dick Walker, for Walker worked in the development team on the radar project at Farnborough and cast a line in some of the local waters, although as far as I know he never went to Frensham Ponds. However, Bill Raison who'd started his successful tackle shop business in the locality some years before the war told me of the occasions Dick came to his shop. Bill knew he was an experienced angler, one who talked of fly tying at length as well as coarse fishing.

It was deemed that the ponds gave a good ground indication to this general area and would perhaps be a marker to London, hence from 1940 until 1947 the land which formed the ponds lay fallow. Perhaps that gives the wrong expression, for nature takes it course, war or no war. In the smaller of the two ponds – which as this story unfolds will become the main topic – the lake bed, which was fertile ground, became a haven for young pine trees. They grew well and as they were unmolested they developed into a small forest, most of them reaching a height of 10ft or so.

When the war came to an end, plans to reflood the area were made, and it's here that we come across the first problem with the water. I had originally understood that Polish refugees were given the job to clear the small pine forest, but information gained recently by my friend Dick Gayner has put me in touch with Les Bonner, who tells me that a small local company for whom he worked did the job. Unfortunately however, they left a legacy, for when the task was finished masses of tree stumps were left. Instead of uprooting the infant saplings, they cut the young trees off some 18in from the ground. This would cause big problems. Detailed plumbing by friends and myself carried out during our actual fishing at Frensham Little Pond has showed that certain areas are worse than others, but with one or two places completely clear. However, the carp understandably rather like the snaggy spots!

After flooding, both lakes were left somewhat to their own devices from 1947 until 1952. However, all was about to change, for besides other fish transfers and purchases the all-important modern carp stockings took place in November of 1952.

Over 100 little carp (one year olds) were purchased from the Surrey Trout Farm. Why carp were purchased and stocked into both of Frensham's ponds at the time remains a mystery – unless I'm doing someone down, in the early 1950s the movement to stock with carp as a sporting species was in its embryonic stage. But whatever the reason, the foresight of this move was to yield exciting consequences some twenty years later.

Sadly, I've never been able to trace through the local angling club how this stocking came about. However, as the lakes were close to the main Surrey Trout Farm headquarters at Haslemere, delivery would almost certainly have been made by Donald Leney himself. His big shooting-brake car with a trailer attached to hold the tubs which were protected by wicker basketwork would have had a bumpy journey. With unmade roads around the general area of the lakes the little carp must have wondered where they were heading for. At least the journey was short – unlike those of some of their brethren who sometimes experienced long train escapades to far-reaching parts of the country! It was on a day in March 1952 that the carp were released into the ponds, darting away into the steely-blue, clear, shallow water. It would be years before they would see what Frensham looked like from the bank again!

I've said that both waters were stocked, but it appears that the Little Pond received the greater amount – 100 of the yearlings were placed in its waters and the remaining into the Big Pond. As with many of 'Leney' stockings, the bulk of the carp were either mirrors or leathers with all the variations in between, but very few all-scalers (common carp) resulted. This was the case with most supplies that Donald Leney brought back from the fish farm he dealt with in northern Holland. With the Frensham stockings, just a few common carp were present.

Fishing had taken place at Frensham throughout the years since the war, with rudd and tench flourishing; also present were pike and perch. The shallow, clear water contained plenty of food and saw to it that the fish grew. So did the tiny carp! As far as I can tell they were never fished for; indeed in the 1950s few people fished for carp at all. It was going to be a score of years or more before their presence was felt and the tremendous potential realized.

## TOPOGRAPHY

Perhaps now is the time to give a more detailed insight into the topography of the lakes. Both were shallow with a depth no greater than 6–7ft. The bottom of the Little Pond in places was strangely undulating as it seemed you could wade through the water, then suddenly step up on to a tussock, step off it again, and so on. The southern shoreline in the area of the Reeds swims was especially like this. The reeds which grew in profusion around the greater part of the water added very much to the overall beauty. Neither lake, however, supported much in the way of weed, other than small patches dotted here and there. One corner of the Little Pond was different, for by the original boat house in the north-east corner grew a profusion of water lilies. Plenty of

*Sand and shallow water
means it is time for bathing.*

swims were available, although long-distance casting could tie up an area, especially if a number of anglers were fishing close together.

The most readily definable feature both lakes boasted was sand. Yes, fine yellow sand and lots of it – so much so in fact, that the Surrey and Hampshire locals treated the whole area as an inland 'seaside spot'. The gently sloping banks which led out into shallow water made it ideal for family picnic trips. Today, and more than ever when the sun is out, Frensham looks like a day on Brighton beach. Here was fishing problem number two, for although hot days produced big crowds, inevitably so did the nights. The goings-on at the Little Pond that sometimes accom-panied darkness provided a constant embarrassment to carpmen who were sitting quietly by their rods!

During the 1960s the carp at Frensham survived the life-threatening shock of that frightening winter England endured during 1962/3. I talked of this icy blast during the Redmire chapter – it decimated fish stocks the length and breadth of the land as lakes were encapsulated in solid ice for some three months. Somehow, and I can't begin to understand how, the Frensham carp survived. The shallow water and soft lake bed that perhaps hid freshwater streams some-how had enough life-giving oxygen within them to help the fish survive this ordeal. I haven't met anyone over these last few years who can remember if any carp were found dead at the water after this bad winter. You'll know why the bulk of the carp survived as the story continues...

The 1960s slipped by with little to report from either of the ponds, other than the fact that they were both classified as general coarse fisheries. It seems that pike grew beyond average size at the Big Lake, with the tench and rudd fishing well in the Little Pond. I'm sure, of course, that some carp were certainly hooked if not landed during this period, but I can't find any such reports or people to confirm this – unless you know different!

I shall now come forward in time to around 1972 when carp anglers as such arrived on the scene at Frensham Little Pond.

Both Bob Burchett and Alan Barker were among the first to fish for the carp. Originally, Bob was fishing another local Farnham stillwater until it was closed for dredging purposes. Along with Alan he went to Frensham and found the carp comparatively easy to catch! Both would go for an evening's 'crust' fishing. The carp were by then into double figures and Bob remembers that one overnight session resulted in eight fish.

*Beautiful young Leney carp captured from Frensham in the late 1960s.*

*One of the many snags, a legacy left from when the pond was reflooded after the war.*

*Dick Gayner foulhooked this glorious twenty-one-pounder in 1975.*

Around this time the water also attracted a small band of carp anglers hailing from the south coast town of Portsmouth. Two of the regulars were brothers, Rick and Dave Jones, and these two caught many fine carp from Frensham over the years. At a guess, they also had the longest unbroken run of carp fishing at the water.

In 1974 the National Trust took over the water, along with the surrounding land, although the Farnham Angling Club still had full access to the fishing and bailiffed the area through the efforts of the infamous Mr and Mrs Hack.

And the carp appeared to be getting bigger – Rick Jones banked a super 26-pounder around 1973, Alan Barker had a 22lb mirror in 1974, Dick Gayner foulhooked a glorious 21lb mirror in the dorsal with a spinner around 1975,

and Bob Burchett caught two lovely looking mirrors of 20lb 8oz and 23lb 8oz in 1976. This group of anglers had the fishing more or less to themselves, and in truth kept it very quiet! After all, people like me might have got to hear about it!

Towards the end of the 1970s the great 'peanut boom' transpired at Frensham, and as on many waters this bait proved to be devastating. By then other local carp anglers were in on the action. One angler, Kevin Grozier, caught what I think might have been the first carp over 20lb at Frensham on a floating bait – crust. It was to be a bonanza period with many big fish starting to get caught, including the first genuine 30lb carp. I believe John Ferris landed two over the magic weight around the 1981 period, the biggest being

*Bob Burchett, an early Frensham angler, with a twenty-pounder taken in 1975.*

32lb. Also, although it would be some years before I found this out, the National Association of Specialist Anglers' (NASA) top carp of 1982 was a 35lb monster from Frensham. Portsmouth lad Dave Jones also caught a 30lb-plus fish at this time. These big carp collectively represented very big fish for the Surrey area, and the anglers concerned were understandably keen not to have the Little Pond at Frensham overrun with every Tom, Dick or Harry who claimed he was a carp angler.

But secrets always get out in the end, and during the 1980s the pressure really started. To put things in perspective, what you might not realize is that Surrey's number one attraction these days, Yateley, hadn't yet properly surfaced at the time. Believe me, Frensham Little Pond was very important as a big carp fishery.

*Kevin Grozier with a tremendous mirror landed in 1981 on floating crust.*

## PERSONAL EXPERIENCES

Now I come to the period in time in the Frensham carp story that I can tell personally, for I originally stumbled on its potential with the help of Chris Yates. Let me explain. Shortly after Chris landed the new record carp at Redmire Pool in 1980 he struck up a relationship with Donald Leney himself. Chris met with Donald every so often at Donald's beautiful Haslemere residence, and here the talk was of carp, Redmire and other waters that Donald had stocked over the long years that the Surrey Trout Farm had been in business.

Donald then lent Chris invoice books of his fish-stocking transactions. Chris showed me these volumes and the following close season we set forth to discover some of the more local venues. We found Frensham, the Army Lake and several others of note within the pages, and we ventured to some. In fact, I visited the Little Pond during the late summer of 1982. Once there I found an angler who was all set up for carp fishing, but when I enquired he reckoned he was eel fishing! The conversation went something like this.

'Any luck yet?' I said, looking hopeful.

'No,' said the serious-looking angler.

'Much been caught here lately?' I added.

He turned and looked at me. 'A few eels,' he said quietly.

'No carp then?' I retorted.

'Someone had a bream the other day,' he said.

'Looks like a good water for carp though,' I said, trying to press the point.

'There's good eels here,' he said, looking slightly uneasy and disinterested.

The trouble was I knew he was carping, and he also knew that I knew…!

But the best was yet to come, for when I visited the NASA conference at Reading in the close season of 1983 Chris Yates introduced me to some anglers he knew were fishing the water, and I bet they thanked him a bunch for that! When I popped the question, they just stared and looked through me as though I wasn't there. Then when I asked the question again, the reception became slightly hostile. From then on it looked to be a waste of time, for it was obvious I was going to get no help from them. Little did they know that these actions made me more determined to find out…so with the new season less than two months away, plans started to be formalized.

The decision was made, in my mind anyway, for it seemed Frensham held many secrets – secrets I wanted to find out about. I became so embroiled with the thought of these carp which I knew were 'Leney' fish that my enthusiasm rubbed off on my immediate fishing buddies, Jan Wenczka and Terry Glebioska. I guess that the circumstantial evidence combined with the whispers we'd heard had put them in a frame of mind to join me.

There are advantages in a small group of friends fishing together, for it became possible to keep an eye on the water for most of the week. As I lived closest to the water I elected to bait up for us during the week, with Jan and Terry coming at the weekend.

### Bait and Tactics

Some of my friends helped on the subjects of bait and tactics. Andy Little, who knew of the water, recommended a boiled bait. It was made up of high-protein ingredients such as casein, sodium caseinate, lactalbumin and vitamins and minerals. Bob James tipped me the wink on the Richworth flavour that was destroying many waters (this was the 'cheese' one) and we used a sweetener at the rate 5ml to the 12oz mix. Finally, we dyed the boilies deep red. The finished bait, approximately 18mm in size, was perfect not only in smell and texture but in taste as well.

The hookbaits themselves were made buoyant, either by rolling the mixture around cork or polystyrene balls or later by microwaving them! The end rig was comparatively new at the time, the super buoyant bait being held down straight off a 2oz lead – what we would call a pop-up these days. The hooklink was monofilament 8lb in strength and around 6in in length. There was no hair rig, just the time-honoured bolt rig with the hook proud of the bait. Finally, the line was pulled back super tight in line clips.

*On the look-out – fishing from the beach area in 1983.*

We busied ourselves making plenty of this bait, and during the latter half of April and then through May the baiting campaign commenced. I was sure the carp would find this concoction to their liking – now, with the benefit of hindsight, it appears that high-protein boilies hadn't been used at the pond before and neither for that matter had the carp seen a pop-up bait!

When the weather became warmer in May the carp started to show themselves. Wow...I'd never seen anything like it in my life. Some of them looked perfect monsters as they reared up on their tails way out in the open water. The Lily Pad bay, adjacent to the boat house cottage where Cyril Jollands (the National Trust warden) and his wife lived, also revealed the carp lying up in still, warm conditions. Here a convenient tree hung out over the water, and the fish I saw from this viewpoint convinced me that carp of over 30lb lived in Frensham. Besides my estimated weight of these carp, it was the length of these fish that was something new to me. I spied several which looked 3ft long, honest! The scaling of these fish was also spectacular. Some looked like extremely heavily scaled mirrors while others looked near linear mirrors – having one row of identically sized mirror scales perfectly aligned along the lateral line.

Collectively, I spent some considerable time perched up in this tree, and when I threw some of our bait into this area the carp ate it! Standing on their heads the carp soon coloured the water – again, the size of the tails on some of these fish was amazing. Every now and then one would flap on its side in a sudden burst along the bottom as feeding carp often do. The slab-sided depth, all golden-brown with the faintest hint of red, would show up momentarily to make my blood race through my veins. With their sleek looks, steely-blue backs and huge fins they represented something that was so enormously desirable…

I don't think there was ever a time when I was more happy with my fishing, for here was a water close to home that held a fair head of beautiful big carp with some of them clearly over 30lb in weight and who knows what else. It was all too good to be true, so something just had to go wrong. It did…with the season just a few days away Jan, Terry and I realized we were far from welcome on the water. Somehow all the night tickets (ten in all) for the first night had been booked up the instant they were made available, so we would have to wait until dawn on opening day at the earliest. I won't bore you with the many other similar instances that took place during the first two years at the lake, suffice it to say that if the fish hadn't been so beautiful and we hadn't caught any of them I'd have jacked it in!

## THE FIRST CAST!

That first session in which Jan and I fished from noon to dusk provided our first chance of a fish! We'd positioned ourselves on the south bank nearly opposite the beach area. At about 4 p.m. without further ado, my line on the left-hand rod suddenly shot away. I was dozing at the time, but I heaved into the fast-running carp, for without doubt this was what I was attached to. All too soon the line went solid, and no matter how hard I pulled it wouldn't move. In the end, the line broke and so did my heart. The first run – and a lost 'Leney' carp. After this – for the next few days for me anyway – it was back to work, but Jan and Terry returned.

The following day I raced away from work with the wind in my tail. It must have been 5 p.m. before I drew up in the car-park. I knew that Jan had intended to fish the beach area, and I rushed up through the beautiful pine forest and then down towards the vast expanse of water. From yards away I could see Jan sitting behind his rods.

By then I was sprinting – complete with business suit and best shoes! When I was clear of the trees and on the sand my activities drew Jan's attention. 'Hello mate, what's happened?' I said, panting. But before he could reply I'd spotted the wet carp sack hung out over the reeds.

'We're off the mark, and a twenty too,' Jan beamed. It transpired that a run had come in the early morning light.

'Well done, mate,' I said, adding, 'How big?'

Jan turned and smiled. '25lb,' he said. 'Mind you Chris, I wouldn't call it a good-looking fish. It looks a bit like other 25-pounders we've caught from elsewhere – a bit gutty, you know.'

Never mind that, the carp were on the bait and the anticipation of what might be in store for us made my heart beat more than it should have.

The next morning Jan had another bite. This time the carp roared off in amongst the snags (sunken pine trees), but with skill he extracted it and when he had done so it was plain sailing to the net. This fish was more like it – a fabulous looking double-row linear of just under 25lb. Unfortunately, I missed seeing this fish as well – how I hate work – but it was a spectacular 'Leney' with a length of 32in to the fork of the tail and totally unmarked. Terry then opened his account with another beauty of just over 25lb the following day. As can be seen, the weight of these first fish were much of a muchness – and so it turned out to be, for we found that they grew to an average weight of around 25lb.

By then free from work, I was able to sit in anticipation for several early mornings' fishing from the 'beach'. Carp were in evidence, either jumping clear of the water or rolling heavily some 80–100yd out from the shoreline. I could cast to them easily, having once waded out some 10yd or so and then punching the lead hard to the distant mark. The groundbait was put out using a wrist rocket (a high-tech catapult) which became a godsend to carp anglers who wished to fish and more importantly bait far off. The incredible line clips that we'd bound tightly to the rod just above the ferrule could hold the line so tight that a passing bird could land on it and almost play a tune! Although this set-up looked strange there can be no denying its effectiveness, and once we were catching most other people copied the style.

Frensham would often lie quiet in the early morning air, being isolated from road or flight path, and save for the odd muffled disturbance of a dog walker or solitary jogger it was as perfect as it could be. The beach area gave a good view of almost the whole vista of the water, though mist would often be in evidence to spoil this view. Rising as if from a witch's cauldron, silent and menacing, it would seemingly wrap itself around one's person. I can almost feel this sensation as I write, and it seemed to heighten the effect of fishing for these carp. Imagine, if you can, this vast open area of water lying in front of you and covered in mist that was constantly changing, moving around as if a huge unseen hand was slowly stirring it about. Little wonder that men like me wanted to fish at Frensham for its carp!

## A CATCH TO REMEMBER

My chance of a carp came within a week. The run came shortly after 7.30 a.m. and I'd been at the lake since first light – I'd managed these sessions twice a week before work. The lasting memory of that fish, however, was the bite itself! When you use the method of bolt rig with the line drawn tightly back into a line clip it produces the most amazing carp runs.

I was dozing again, so I never saw the rod tip pull hard round as the pressure built up before the line shot out of the line clip and the bobbin cavorted crazily up and down the indicator needle. Because of the long range at which I was fishing, I picked up the rod and reeled like fury trying to make contact. The line feathered up out of the water in a huge sweeping arc, and several seconds later I made solid contact with the fish. A plume of water shot high into the air as the fish responded to the pressure – a spectacular sight.

After some time it came much closer, and with me out in the water near the tops of my waders the carp went in the net. This turned out to be a great long brute of a fish, a terrific looking carp that turned the scales at 24lb 8oz. Looking care-

fully at this beautiful carp, there seemed not to be a mark on it. Its length was 32in and its girth 25in, making it almost identical in proportion to Redmire carp of the same size.

My dream of coming into contact with the genuine, awe-inspiring 'Leney' carp was coming to life…but I wanted to catch more and larger ones!

Shortly after this catch, a further run produced a carp that snagged me far out in the pine forest! After this it was time to leave for work, but with the action I had had I eagerly made plans to return the following week. These early morning sessions saw the best feeding period and also gave us the chance to fish for three or four hours before the day-trippers would arrive. A friend, Steve Neville, who also fished the water coined the expression that Frensham looked just like Burton-on-Sea on a sunny day. This name later became abbreviated to just 'Burton', and we always used that name afterwards.

The next trip saw all three of us – Terry, Jan and myself – fish together in the beach area as the bulk of our baiting was now centred in this spot. Terry had the first run of the day – by then we were expecting runs as the fish were really on the bait. Terry's fish went off at such a pace that the rod was rattling in the rest before he even picked it up. He heaved like mad but to no avail, almost straight away it was stuck fast in a snag. Eventually he wound in…the hooklink had broken. Then Jan, who'd never left his rods since first light, suddenly shot up and grabbed a rod before the line was out of the clip. Immediately he had the upper hand as this carp stayed clear of the snags. Soon both of us were out in the water, Jan with a bent rod and me by his side with the net – my net in fact. However, after we'd caught our first sight of the carp, Jan sent me back to get his larger net!

This fish looked like a monster as Jan held it on a tight line, and my God, it was a monster! When we looked in the bottom of the net, we both said, 'Thirty pounds!' However, the weight this fish registered on the scales was largely due to its huge gut. I'm sure it was full of spawn and although looking perfectly healthy in every other

*Unknown fish, from an unknown water – 31lb 2oz!*

respect we treated it very carefully after weighing the fat lady in at 33lb 4oz.

Two days later, come dawn, the three of us were back on the beach again. On this July morning Frensham was shrouded in mist, and although we could see little we could certainly hear the muffled sounds as carp after carp threw themselves out of the water.

Wading out to the top of my waders I let fly with the lead; somewhere out into the mist I heard it 'plop'. It was only an hour before my left-hand rod signalled a run. The fish battled far off out in the misty dawn water, but eventually we landed it and at 23lb 2oz it was a good start. This carp again displayed classical lines, being 31in long and 25in in girth. The same rod sprang back into life thirty minutes later. After another terrific scrap an even bigger fish came ashore – 26lb 12oz! A further cast, yet again with the same rod, produced within ten minutes an almighty wrench on the rod top. This fight was uncertain for some time. At one stage the pressure was terrific with the rod bent double as the carp was making for the snags and looked as though it might win! Lady Luck, however, was with me again and eventually I got the upper hand. Soon it came into shallow water. Almighty swirling vortices were in evidence as I played the carp

much more carefully – this had to be a really big one!

Terry, who by now had waded out into the water with the net, turned round with a big grin on his face! 'It's a whopper, Chris,' he shouted as he scooped the carp up into the net. We rushed out to see Terry as he brought the net ashore. When he put it down, we all stared in disbelief. What a fish...tremendous length, huge head and huge fins. It sparkled in the morning light – along with my eyes! My third fish of the session, and my first 30lb carp!

The carp was an unknown fish from an unknown water and a genuine home-grown 'Leney' thirty-pounder. At 31lb 2oz it brought the morning's total of three fish to exactly 81lb! Every now and then most carp anglers have their day...undoubtedly, this was mine!

By then we had caught two 30lb carp in three days! Fabulous fishing, but something that brought us grief from some of the resident carp anglers! Some of the stories they told about us were good enough for the *Sunday Sport,* needless to say they were untrue and we took no notice.

As the year progressed Jan and I continued to catch many superb carp, nearly all of them weighing over 20lb. Poor old Terry suffered at the hands of fate, however, as fish after fish either became snagged, the hook pulled or some other catastrophe happened. For instance, at one stage Terry had some duff line. He lost a fish one morning, and on testing his line afterwards he found that the 10lb line was breaking at 5lb! By his next visit he'd changed the brand, but all too soon his line was again caught on a snag and Terry proceeded to show us all how good the new line was. Hooping the rod round he said: 'Look, I told you this was good stuff,' as he heaved against the snag...then the rod broke!

On another occasion he arrived with some new leads – the fluted type that were supposed to come up quickly from the bottom on the retrieve. Terry told us: 'These will sort out the snags, fly over the top they will, you'll all be using them as soon as you see how good they are.' But during Terry's three-day session he lost them all!

## A NEW RECRUIT!

The next season (1984) started with a new recruit joining us, the noted Andy Little. If you don't know, then believe me when I say that he's a fishing machine. I'd talked to Andy at length about the fish losses in the snags. I thought he might have some answers for us. Sadly, I have to report that he suffered from the snags as much as we did, and it took thirteen runs before he at last landed a carp. That first carp was a cracker – extremely heavily scaled, dark bronze in colour and weighing in at just over 20lb. Andy had a smile from ear to ear, more with relief than anything else.

Of the events that took place that year, several are worth recounting. On opening day Jan banked a big fish of just under 30lb. It was a

*A beautifully shaped, near linear mirror for Jan Wenczka – 1983.*

*A big linear for Jan on opening day.*

tremendous looking carp that had a continuous unbroken row of large scales completely along its lateral line. Many carp anglers would have given their eye teeth for a fish such as this. I prepared to photograph this catch, but no sooner had I taken one picture when Jan proclaimed that things weren't right. He put the fish down, carefully covering it with a wet sack, raced off and then returned...with his hat on!

Another occasion saw us fishing the Reeds area. Jan had a run, but the fish had a head start and eventually got stuck round a buoy – several of these were placed in the lake at this point. He said he was going in after it. Off he went with the landing net tucked up under one arm and his rod in the other. Soon he arrived at the buoy and could see that the line was hopelessly tangled. Upon further investigation, however, he found the end which was attached to the fish. Gingerly, he pulled it. It moved – quickly he broke the line on either side of the buoy, tied a quick double granny and wound the line as fast as he could on to the reel. Surprisingly enough, the line didn't shoot out into open water as we thought it would, but disappeared way off to the left, ending at... the next buoy! Jan waded along and there, tight on the surface up against the floating obstacle, lay his carp. He simply scooped it up, saying, 'That'll do!' At 28lb 12oz he wasn't complaining! The fish was 3ft in length and extremely impressive to look at.

I too had a similar experience. A storming run resulting from a long cast had the fish always going to the right like a steam train, and I was powerless to stop it kiting behind another buoy. As with Jan's fish it became stuck solid. I was wearing chest waders, so giving the rod to Jan and feeding the line through my fingers I followed its path. I lifted the buoy and, would you believe it, the line went round once, then it went round again: this carp had somehow swum a complete circle – twice! When I released the line it fell limp. With trepidation I pulled it, and it moved. There was then a big swirl as the fish exploded on the surface virtually in my arms, and I hand-lined it into the net – just a bit lucky! Arriving back on the bank, we weighed this super mirror in at 23lb.

A little later another run came to the same rod with the bait placed in almost the same spot as before. But this time I put heavy pressure on the fish and always had the upper hand. That said, this carp gave a good account of itself with heavy, boring runs which were hard to check. With Jan by my side, we caught a glimpse of the fish as it rolled close to the net – it was a common! Once on the bank it looked magnificent, in fact it was gleaming! Though I thought it might make the magic 20lb figure it fell well short, but I was pleased all the same when Jan announced 18lb 8oz. A nice brace, and from a difficult swim.

But the hard-luck story of the year must have been when Andy hooked a fish from the beach area. On a long line this fish kited way off to the right while Andy was out from the shore up to the tops of his waders in the water. After some time the fish looked like beaching itself, but some 60yd further down the bank. Can you believe that this fish actually did just that, and that it got so far on to dry land that it fell over on its side? Andy splashed his way through the water after it, but another carp angler who was set up between Andy and the fish shouted over that he could net it if Andy wanted. When this angler approached the fish (which was a good one) it suddenly panicked and, splashing around in a frenzy, it righted itself, found the depth of water to just cover itself, then shot off at an incredible rate. Within a minute it got stuck on a snag some 50yd out in the lake and Andy lost it! Remember, at one stage this fish was as near as damn it on the bank! Oh, cruel world.

Andy Little did, however, get his own back, and in a big way, while at the same time our little band of anglers found unprecedented Frensham action in the depths of winter. I'm only glad we did, for our days at Frensham were fast coming to an end...but more of this later as our story unfolds.

One afternoon in early September found me on the banks of Burton yet again. The weather, typical of that time of the year, was warm and windless but with the hint of an edge to it. By then the fish were forced way out into the snags, mainly out from the beach area. Longrange

*Andy Little finally gets one…after this he couldn't stop catching them!*

casting could present a bait to them but the losses were unacceptable…and still people persisted. I tried fishing further along the beach on the edge of the worst area, however, and to the right there lay a vast area where the water became shallower up to the western shore. This part of the lake generally saw little activity from the carp, but this day proved the exception as fish after fish showed themselves in a frenzied display of feeding. It proved to be the chink in the armour we were looking for…

Almost straight away, as soon as I moved the rods, a short cast into the midst of this area produced a sizzling run and some ten minutes later I netted the fish. Once ashore I parted the net and here was one of the famed Burton fish, the most perfect carp I've seen or caught – a magnificent 'Leney' linear. What a fish it was; it personified everything a Leney was and it turned the scales at 24lb.

The following afternoon I rushed back again – and there were carp all over the place. Carefully casting back into the same area line bites started almost at once. I stood by the rods all expectant, and remained so for two hours! Reeling in to check the baits I noticed a bit of weed had hidden the hookpoint, but closer inspection actually showed this weed to be a bloodworm impaled on the bare hookpoint. Later I managed two at a time – as you will realise I was using the hair rig.

The carp continued to plunder this newfound explosion of food. As the afternoon wore on so eventually the line raced away. After a short struggle in came a weird looking carp of 14lb, pale coloured with head features which made it look like it had run into a brick wall at some time during its life. It made me wonder how the hell it came to be in Burton. As I

*One of the most perfect fish I'd ever seen!*

*Steve Temple with a magnificent double-row linear – pure magic!*

pondered over this fish the other rod was away. This fish too turned the scales at under 20lb, the smallest brace we'd caught at Burton. With this success I was on the telephone to Andy, for he'd been away from Burton for a while. Wasting no time at all, Andy journeyed forth the following day, but the session was dogged with frustration as the fish gorged themselves on the natural food and ignored his! At the weekend we talked over

the problem, and by the following day Andy had hatched a plan.

What followed proved to be one of the few times in all the carp fishing I've done where bait made such a difference to one's catches, above anyone else fishing at the time.

All these years later I'm still not quite convinced about Andy's explanation of the magic bait he produced. The concept was to produce a

*After losing several big carp, Ron Buss put this superb thirty-pounder on the bank.*

boilie that the fish would eat while at the same time they would continue to dig in the blood-worm beds. But how? The answer was a dissolving insect-based bait! You see, Andy's theory was that if we bombarded the area with this bait, within an hour or two when it was dissolved it would be out there in such quantities that the carp would take in great mouthfuls of the stuff with the bloodworm. He told me some of the boilie ingredients included things such as ants, crustaceans and the like! You could observe what happened to this bait once in the water by placing a boilie in a jam jar full of water. After an hour you would notice it dissolving, and after a further thirty minutes all that was left of the bait was a pyramid-type structure of the contents. This sounds quite technical, but did it work? Well, just listen to this...

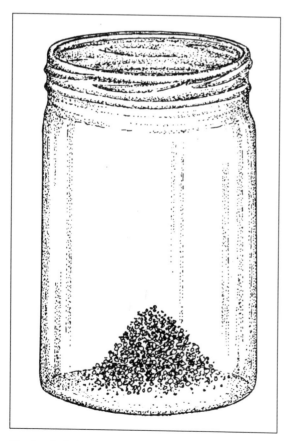

*Testing Andy Little's dissolving bait.*

Over the next few weeks, Andy fished Friday night to Sunday morning, and his catches – from an area with no snags – quite frankly took your breath away. Included amongst these fabulous hauls were several fish which we'd never seen before: cracking linear mirrors, super heavily scaled mirrors and, to top it all a common over 20lb that looked like something out of Redmire. One fish in particular was another three-footer (36in in length) and one which I'd never seen. The carp were on the bait so much that Andy captured the same carp from the same spot *three* times in as many weekends! Naturally, all these fish picked up the bait before it dissolved – in other words, sixty to ninety minutes after casting out. It was some of the most impressive fish-catching action that Burton had ever seen, and Andy made the most of it. I believe he didn't lose one carp during this period. The bait worked superbly and Andy's tactics were spot on.

The end rig he was using was somewhat different from what we had started out with a couple of years before. The 2oz bomb was stopped by a small swivel to which the hooklink was also tied. This hook line was 6lb line and almost 3ft in length. The indicators – at the rod end – were light and no line clips were used. In fact, this is what is called a confidence rig. The runs were sometimes jerky but always developed into confident bites that were unmissable. The hooks were Drennan Super Specialists (then comparatively new), and the hair length was around 1in. As mentioned earlier, with this general area of the pond being free from snags all Andy had to do was play a carp in the conventional way. That said, he had some memorable battles with these quite superb big carp. This kind of action when no one else was catching drew some attention. The plain fact was that other people were tearing their hair out – one chap who was there most weekends and fished in the same general area as Andy was getting somewhat cheesed off, and that's putting it mildly. After Andy landed the big common this chap came round to witness and photograph it. Andy could see the look in his eyes as this fellow stared at yet another big carp caught from under his nose. Andy then gave him one

*One of many that fell to the special dissolving bait.*

bait – just the one – he cast it out and within twenty minutes in came a 30lb mirror. Was this chap convinced or what! Andy didn't give him another bait, not that the captor minded for as far as he was concerned Andy was a magician!

At this time Steve Neville captured an outstanding fish – 28lb of fully-scaled mirror which at the time was one of the largest ever recorded in the UK! This carp was caught from way down near the dam and came after a concerted effort by Steve and his friend Kevin O'Farrol in fishing this area. They undertook a big baiting campaign with boilies, and several fish had fallen by the time Steve caught the magnificent fully-scaled carp. The only sad part of this capture was the photographs. Let me explain. This run had come in the early evening, an evening that was wet in the extreme. Steve was on his own during this

*Jan Wenczka shows a 3ft Frensham carp to the camera.*

*Dave Jones, one of the original band of carp fishers at Frensham, with a super 24lb common. Few were present at the time of the stocking.*

session as Kevin O'Farrol was away at another lake. To Steve's credit, he hooked, played and landed the big fish all on his own.

Once he had unhooked the carp and placed it in a sack, he went off up the bank and found Andy Little. The rain was still tipping down and Steve was keen not to keep the big carp in the sack any longer than was necessary. They both agreed to photograph it straight away under Steve's big umbrella. Sadly, however, the flash-light photographs were far from clear. As luck would have it Andy's own camera, normally a good picture-taker, was on the blink at the time! Never mind about the pictures though, shining a torch on the fish made both anglers eyes sparkle as they looked down at this marvellous big carp. It had to be one of the most beautiful in all of England, and was one carp that I had a burning

*What can you say about such a fish? It's little wonder that Frensham carp dominated some people's lives so.*

ambition to see on the end of my line. When I heard of the capture (too late to see the fish personally) I knew that it was a special carp. Andy's description of being in the presence of this fish, of touching it and cradling it made the hairs on the back of my neck bristle in a peculiar fashion. Such is the way big carp can effect you.

Eventually, as winter took its grip on the year, the action faded away, and as the fish moved so did we anglers.

## COLD-WATER CARP

Winter carp fishing at Burton was not, I think, and had never been a practised art. So what drew Andy to its banks one bitterly cold December afternoon I'll never know – I for one had never thought of the water as one to fish in the colder months. But as the light faded so Mr Little's buzzer sounded! In came a 19lb common carp. That's not all, for he reported carp throwing

*Steve Neville will probably never catch a more beautiful carp than this – 28lb of fully-scaled mirror!*

themselves out of the water all over the place and concentrated around the old bloodworm area to the right of the beach.

I hastily arranged to go the next afternoon, even though the weather was still very cold, and Jan also decided to join us. As luck would have it, however, I got held up in London so it was late afternoon before I crunched my way along the sandy beach area. Both Jan and Andy were already installed, fishing adjacent swims. Looking at the spot there seemed little room for me, so I decided to walk round to the far opposite bank and fish back into the same general area. It took fifteen minutes to get to this spot. Puffing and panting and with aching legs I eventually arrived, slumping down in a heap on the ground. However, soon all was set.

I cast out spot on! I had just put my bottom down on the small seat when a buzzer sounded – but it wasn't mine. Looking out over the darkened water I could see Jan wading out with his rod bent, and soon Andy was by his side. After a spirited fight a cheer went up as the fish was netted. Then after a pause Jan shouted over, 'It's a cracker, come and have a look.'

I reeled in, retraced my footsteps and eventually appeared back where the carp fishing duo were gathered. The fish had already been weighed in at 26lb. It *was* a beautiful fish – red and gold showed along the vast flanks as they displayed a totally unmarked finish.

'That'll do for me,' I thought as I made my way back. Twenty minutes later I was casting my tackle back out into the lake. Almost straight away a buzzer sounded – again it wasn't mine. I looked over to see Jan once again with a bent rod in his hand! Andy was by his side with the net, then another buzzer sounded. I heard Andy say 'Its gone through my line.' Who was he kidding? The buzzer was going berserk – just a continuous high-pitched tone. Within seconds Andy realized he had a run as well! I could just make him out trying to run through the water back to where his rods were – it was like a film of a runner in slow-motion!

After a lapse of some thirty seconds or so he reached the rod. The line was all gone right down to the knot on the spool, and the rod tip was pulled round at an acute angle! With all this hubbub going on I just had to assist my mates, didn't I? This time I virtually ran the half mile – in a one-piece suit and at my age too! When I finally got there Jan had landed his fish, but Andy was still steadfastly playing his. I remember standing next to Andy with the net, and what with him panting heavily and me wheezing while trying to

*The tremendous length of this autumn-caught fish is clearly shown.*

catch my breath we sounded like a couple of old-age pensioners!

This carp also found its way into the landing net. It must have run out over 150yd of line in its bid for freedom, and although it went through some of the most snaggy areas of the pond, can you believe that it never got stuck once! Indeed, it was a very lucky Mr Little on this occasion.

I took the photos of the two smiling captors each with a carp in their arms while trying to smile myself – this was a job though through the tears.

So, within twenty minutes three big carp had made a mistake, and this action in the middle of December! It just goes to show what observation, application and good angling can achieve on a water that no one had ever thought of casting a line into during the winter. But that was secondary in my mind at that time for I wanted to catch one – after all Jan was beginning to get greedy, two in twenty minutes…

Yet again I trudged back to my far-off pitch. It was dark as I cast the baits out. This time all was quiet for some time, then a buzzer sounded…*it was mine!*

I rushed up to find the line on the right-hand rod streaming out. I struck, the rod hooped over, then suddenly the pressure eased – the fish was cunningly running towards me – and I wound like fury. The winding ended with a fish splashing around in shallow water in front of me. During this time I could hear the lads asking me, 'Do you want any help Chris?' and saying 'Well done, it looks like one apiece.' Then I heard Jan saying, 'Chris, Chris what's happening, how big is it?'

In disbelief, when I shone the torch on what was obviously *not* a carp, there was my prize – I'd caught the only chub in the place!

The following evening I returned to Burton. The weather was similar with high pressure and cold, clear air. Fog and mist then came down, and made me shiver as I prepared the tackle. I had the hot spot to myself, my friends having decided to give me a chance and fully expecting me to tell of a great catch. However, although I stood by the rods for over three hours anticipating a run at any time it didn't happen, and I left for home with the feeling that a seemingly golden chance had appeared not to happen for me.

Such is fishing, however, and far from being dejected by the lack of action I couldn't wait to get back. For me though that would not be for a couple of days. The following evening my intrepid pal Jan was back. His luck held, and he recorded an outstanding brace weighing in at

*Winter success for Jan.*

23lb and over 31lb. I went with Mike Starkey to photograph them straight after Jan had rang from the warden's cottage. The thirty-one-pounder was a breath-taking fish to view as Jan carefully laid it down on the frost-covered grass. This capture occurred one week before Christmas Day in 1985 – some Christmas present for Jan!

So ended the winter action. My efforts had nothing to show, but what the heck, I'd witnessed some great catches.

## THE LAST YEAR

The dawning of the 1986 season saw many new faces come to Burton, anglers both young and keen. They found it hard going to start with but by autumn time their persistence won through as they finally started to get some of the hooked fish on the bank. Amongst these carp landed was a terrific looking 'Leney', a double-row linear fish of outstanding beauty. It weighed just over 27lb. Steve, the young chap who captured this particular specimen, was over the moon with this capture – he was on the telephone the same evening telling me of the beauty of the fish. Getting the pictures developed the next day he rushed to my house and we poured over them – this carp was another 'new' fish and was totally perfect.

Kevin O'Farrol was another angler to land yet another superb carp during the summer months, and again I'd never seen this carp either although by a strange coincidence come autumn Kevin caught this same fish again. Each time it was within ounces of the same weight – 26lb 8oz. Alan Melbourne also scored heavily with the Frensham carp, rich rewards for trying so hard. His best fish weighed 27lb 8oz and turned out to be Jan's thirty-pounder of the previous winter.

One morning when Kevin O'Farrol was packing up he noticed a gleaming car pull up on the sand of the beach area! This was unusual in the extreme as cars were not allowed in this area, but was especially so when a camera crew and model turned up as well. This 'campaign' picture appeared in many of the quality Sunday supplements advertising a well-known saloon car!

In yet another instance, a good friend from way back, Mike Starkey, finally got to grips with a Frensham carp, but only after a few disasters. Can you believe that the big fish that Mike landed was another completely new carp to me? At the time it made me wonder just how many carp lived in Frensham – and what else lay in store for we anglers.

But it was late in November of 1986 when a disaster happened. My friend Ron Buss came to see me – I was way up along the bank from Ron – and he reported a large carp in distress in the margins close to his pitch. I went back to look, and sure enough a big mirror was lying almost belly-up. Ron had tried for some while to revive this fish and as soon as I looked at it I knew which fish it was. A pain of despair shot through me as the scaling revealed it to be the super linear I'd banked earlier in the year. No, I thought, a disaster like this just could not happen to such a staggering carp…

We stopped with that fish for ages, but to no avail – it wasn't going to swim away. Reflecting on this later it crossed my mind that there had been a controversial stocking of small carp a few weeks earlier, but I couldn't believe that had anything to do with it. After all, there were fatalities at the pond from time to time, and even though these mainly occurred in the springtime I naively put this death down to just one of those things. Even though neither Ron nor I could find anything obviously wrong with the fish – no sores, spots, wounds or mucus – the fact remained that it died. This carp was not lost forever, however, because that day another friend named Bob Stuart – a master taxidermist – appeared on the banks and took the specimen away. These days this particular specimen is in residence at Ron Buss's home in a glorious glass case. I too have a carved replica of this carp by Brian Mills, but this is not life-size – for that to happen, it would have to be 33in long with a 25in girth!

Within two weeks of this event a couple more carp were found and the alarm bells started to ring. Being very concerned, Andy and I continued to fish and watch the water almost on a daily basis. We managed several big carp, the first of which was a true winter 20lb mirror and again another new fish to me. It came from the general beach area, right along to the left of the snags, and was one of two chances I had within thirty minutes of one another.

The wind was strong that evening as I sat totally alone in the dark; there was no moon, no street lights and no houses to give even the merest hint of light. Frensham was often like this in the winter. When the first run came, it was a screamer as usual. After hours of huddling under the brolly with the collar of the one-piece suit tight up around my throat, I jumped up in a panic. The bobbin was tight up at the top of the needle and the reel handle was a blur by the speed of the run. The hooking arrangement was a running lead and a long 3ft hooklink with a critically balanced hookbait that just floated down ever so slowly. Picking up the rod and bending into this carp on that windy dark evening was thrilling. Pulling up my waders, I splashed out into the water with the rod bucking wildly in my hands. Pressure had to be brought on to the brute but not so much as to put the light hooklink (6lb) under too much strain – even though at this kind of range the stretch in line is enormous.

Eventually, after some fifteen minutes, I had it close while it plunged on the short line. I pushed out the landing net, then without warning the line suddenly got stuck only feet from where I stood. In a flash the line went tighter and tighter with me being able to do little about it – then there was a lunge and the fish was gone! I was furious. Inspecting the line afterwards I found that it was heavily damaged at the spot where it broke off. The next day I inspected this area and found a huge sunken log, and one that had not been there the week before! Almost certainly what had happened was that it had been pushed into the water by enthusiastic weekend revellers and had then sunk – oh, cruel world!

I was still steaming with anger as the indicator signalled another run. Picking up the rod I felt the same tremendous pull which meant I had fortunately hooked another big carp. This time the fight was short lived as I steered the carp well clear of the previous obstacle. Soon it was thumping its broad tail in the bottom of the landing net. What a cracker – all golden and reddish in colour. It turned the scales at 20lb 12oz and more than made up for the earlier disaster. Andy Little very kindly came over and took some photos, and Cyril, the warden, and his wife both came out to see the carp caught by this crazy fisherman on a cold night like this. Andy and I baited up the area before we left. I couldn't wait to return, but that was not to be until early the following week – decorating saw to that!

On the Saturday it was Andy's turn. I will remember that Saturday for the rest of my life – not so much for the whopper that Andy caught, but of the 4 p.m. news on the radio announcing that a bomb had gone off outside the famous Knightsbridge store, Harrods. I was listening to the news when the telephone rang. It was Andy ringing from the warden's cottage. 'You've got to come quick Chris,' Andy said in a breathless voice. 'I've landed a huge great long thing, it might be a thirty pounder.' 'Hang on Andy,' I said, adding, 'I'll be there...quick!'

I made the trip in fifteen minutes flat! There was Andy all smiles. It was almost dark as we walked along the beach area to his pitch. Once there he fetched the carp out of the sack...it was a monster. We weighed it in at 30lb 4oz. Then we took it along to Cyril's cottage and once there took out the cameras. This incredible carp was 36in to the fork of the tail and 26in in girth – truly a 'Leney' wonder. The look of horror on Cyril's wife's face when she saw Andy actually kiss that gorgeous carp on the nose made us all laugh. That lady had secretly thought for years that we carp anglers were mad...now she knew it was true!

That cold-water thirty-pounder caught by Andy Little was the last to fall before the bad weather really started. Then came the ice of winter that locked Burton tight in a cold store for weeks. When the thaw came Andy was the first to fish, and he found an ice-free area that was the first to unlock. As the day progressed he noticed a white shape far out on the surface, then a dog-walker told him that a 'bloody great pike' was washed up down by the dam. Andy quickly went to investigate; needless to say it wasn't a pike, but a big carp. The shape floating out in front of him proved to be another. The panic button was pressed, the water closed down, and people began running around like chickens without heads. Many carp were found as the ice disappeared, but as most were rotten as hell it was realized that they had died before the water became ice-ridden.

In the middle of all this the Thames Water Authority – who were by then co-ordinating matters – arrived one afternoon. They took away three carp, two of which were still alive! Cyril the warden told me, 'One has those great big scales all over it, Chris.' It had to be the huge fully-scaled mirror carp, one of the most desirable carp in the place, or dare I say the country! I quickly went to the TWA headquarters in Guildford, luckily close to home, and the man in charge, Andy Thomas, took me to a large tank out in the enclosure. This event happened towards the end of February 1987, and it was a very cold evening as Andy guided me out the back to where the holding tanks were situated. These tanks were some 15ft square in size and elevated off the ground so the lip was at chest height. Once there he shone a powerful torch over the tank. At once we saw a big carp lying right in the middle. He quickly shone the torch around the tank...where was the fully-scaled mirror? Then as he shone the light in the near right-hand corner – just a few inches from my nose – there lay this big, black, brooding carp. I took the torch and, shining it at an angle, revealed the huge plated scales all along the flank of this fabulous carp. In the circle of light it seemed unreal, but for the slow rhythmic movement of the gills giving the only indication that it was a living wild creature.

That image will stay with me forever. People who fish for carp and who feel passionately about them will know how I felt that evening as I stood close to that magic fish and wondered whether it was to be spared or not...

We went back to the buildings for a welcome cup of tea and Andy showed me the other carp of the three that had been removed. Looking at the remains of this once fine carp I realized straight away that it was the same fish as Andy Little had caught – the thirty-pounder taken just before Christmas. How could life be so cruel? This fish was to be packed and sent off to the freshwater laboratories at Plymouth for examination. Would a cause of death be found? Time would tell.

Both of the two surviving carp had been given an antiseptic dip, and Andy Thomas told me that if they both lasted the next twenty-four hours there was a chance. The next day only the fully-scaled mirror was left, the other fish having expired during the night...

By then my heart and mind were almost empty; this seemingly total loss of irreplaceable carp hung over me so much that little else occupied my thoughts both day and night! I prayed out loud in desperation, 'Please God, don't let this one die, not this one.'

I visited this fish every morning and evening during that week – it was like visiting someone in hospital, and it seemed that things were going well during the following few days. Although the carp moved little in the cold conditions, to me it looked fine. However, upon meeting Andy on Friday evening he reported that matters had taken a turn for the worse. The fish was listing badly and hardly moving at all as we picked it up in the torchlight. We both feared the worst. Come Saturday morning – after an uneasy night of fitful sleep – Andy Thomas and I went down to the tank...floating dead on the surface was the fish.

Suddenly, my mind was full of hatred, hatred and anger for whoever or whatever had made this happen. In truth, all paths led to the introduction of the new fish, for it seemed that these small carp had been carrying something that the old boys could not handle. But how can I be so sure? Well, on the day of the Burton stocking another Farnham club fishery benefited from the same batch. The old resident stock of carp died at that water as well. This whole crazy situation came about because someone thought Frensham needed restocking – where in truth it was the last thing that was needed.

I have here, laid out on the desk of the Carproom as I write, a photographic record of

*'Please God, let this one live.'*

captures of many of the Frensham carp. All told there are some fifty individual captures. This is by no means the complete list of carp that lived in the water, but must constitute most of them. In 1986 (when the new fish were stocked) the original carp were in their thirty-fifth year – just middle-aged. The go-ahead to stock with the new fish was taken because most close seasons saw the demise of the old carp, these mainly being spawn-bound fish. This happens at most waters and, of course, over a period of ten to fifteen years it can make a drastic difference to the stock levels. So why am I complaining when it seems that restocking at Frensham was not going to be a bad thing?

Well, whoever gave the go-ahead, or whoever persuaded the powers that be to spend money on restocking the water had conveniently forgotten that an official stocking had taken place only a few years before in 1981. In fact, these carp were referred to by the carp anglers at Frensham as the TWA fish, the carp having come through the local Thames Water Authority fishery. These carp were handled by Andy Thomas, Assistant Fishery Officer, and stocked by him personally. In all there were some fifty mixed carp, commons and mirrors, all of which were around 2lb in weight. If we take it that some of those fish might not have made it through to becoming sizeable fish, we can see that a substantial restocking had in fact taken place. These carp were smashing little fish and ones that would grow hopefully into big fish in later years. When my friends and I were fishing at Frensham from 1983 onwards, we caught several of these nice small carp. They were then around double figures in weight. When the fish kill happened I believe I can say with some certainty that only a few perished – I myself

*After the disaster, two fish are mounted.*

saw only two brought ashore, although there may well have been more that were never recovered. It's my guess that at least twenty-five of these carp survived...will these grow on to become the next Frensham monsters? I hope so.

Although I told you of the almost total wipe-out of the big Frensham carp, some have sur-vived. Friends who have been back to the water in recent years and some who have fished it tell me there are maybe eight to twelve originals left. The largest, a known carp which was caught at just over 30lb a little time before the disaster, is now approaching 35lb. Another very famous carp is also alive, this being the spectacular look-ing 'double row' linear mirror that used to be caught around the 27lb mark. I believe there could be several carp over 30lb in the water these days, but to people like me it was hard enough to catch the blighters when fifty-odd carp lived in the water, never mind less than a dozen!

Now, as I pen the tragic end to the Frensham carp story, my mind still cannot after all this time work out how those fabulous 'Leney' carp sur-vived everything life had thrown at them in the thirty-five years of their existence – including the terrible winter of 1962/3 – yet something far smaller than a pin-head had killed them. No one has ever given me a convincing reason as to how they died and of what. Desperately, we know so little...

*Two of the best remembered – Kevin O'Farrol and Ron Buss display the spoils of a busy night.*

# 4 BILLING AQUADROME – HOLIDAY FUN AND BIG CARP

*'Second only to Redmire itself.'*

## FIRST NEWS

It was in the summer of 1957 that Billing Aquadrome first hit the angling press headlines. A man named Bob Reynolds caught five carp over 20lb in a single week. This proved yet again that given a fertile water, in this case a fairly large gravel pit, the tiny Leney carp could turn into monsters!

This now-famous lake differs from all the others in this book by being a very public water – in fact, it lay within a virtual holiday-home type atmosphere with caravans and the whole 'camp' being geared towards a family retreat. It was indeed a far cry from the remoteness of Redmire and quietness of Savay. However, these carnival-type surroundings only started to get underway in the early to mid-1960s, for years before this few were allowed to fish – and giant carp swam unhindered and unthreatened by man.

Originally, Billing Aquadrome was stocked with trout by the former owner, Col. Elwes. This took place in the late 1920s, and although there is no doubt that the trout thrived in the clear, clean water they were soon to receive some competition in the shape of king carp! Shortly after, Col. Elwes suddenly left and Sam Mackeness took over the property. Sam has lasted as the owner to this very day, and he has seen some of the cream of carp fishers pass through his gates, all with the firm intent of banking an elusive Billing carp! It was Sam Mackeness who stocked the lake in 1935 with two-year-old Leney fingerlings, the original invoice showing that just forty-three king carp were supplied. These carp were

placed, I believe, into the Willow Tree Lake, this being the largest of six gravel pit extractions on the site.

It was a dark November evening when the fish were delivered to the aquadrome, coming directly by train from the Nailsworth depot and the container being protected by the usual wickerwork basket. Sam picked up the heavy canister from the local railway station and arrived on the banks of the aquadrome as darkness approached. As the fledglings sped away into the dark vastness of water, little did Sam know that he was party to a legend of giant fish that is still with us nearly sixty years later!

Further shipments were made from Leney in December 1936 and 1937, giving all the lakes at Billing a considerable stock of quality carp. Although some of the carp were easy prey for the resident trout stocks, a good percentage of the tiny carp made it through to sizeable fish well capable of holding their own. They grew quickly – often carp pack on weight at an alarming rate if they are stocked into largely virgin waters. The Billing carp were no different and they simply raced away. Only two years later came reports of two carp caught, both double-figure fish and obviously displaying startling growth rates. With few anglers being granted permission to fish, the potential of what Billing had to offer was never realized by the unsuspecting fishing world. The war came shortly afterwards, and all lay fallow and closed at the aquadrome with no angling taking place or visitors allowed in. The growing carp had almost ten years of peace and quiet – that's if you can call the war years quiet!

Come the late 1940s the aquadrome was reopened, but still Sam Mackeness was reluctant to let many anglers fish. Some did, however, and

*'Bob Reynolds fished off a tiny island.'*

in the early 1950s a 16lb mirror was landed by a lucky fisherman, while giant fish to 30lb were found dead from time to time in the Willow Tree Lake, generally in a spawn-bound condition. These gave a clue as to the possible size of fish in the lake. The word started to be passed around locally that Billing Aquadrome held some mysterious uncatchable monster carp...

## HISTORY-MAKING CATCHES

Against this backcloth entered one Bob Reynolds, an angler who had taken up carp fishing a year or two beforehand and who had had success already by landing from a water in the locality fish of 13lb and 10lb. He was meticulous in his fishing and well suited both in skill and guile to outwitting the cautious carp. Like many he'd been inspired by Dick Walker and the exploits of the Carp Catchers' Club. Also, like many up-and-coming anglers of the period Bob was influenced by Dick Walker's record 44lb carp. It made a big impression on many. Bob Reynolds was also an advocate of heavy but controlled groundbaiting, having carried out experiments with both groundbait and hookbaits of identical size. The chance to further experiment became possible when unexpectedly an invitation was offered to fish for one of the big carp in Billing Aquadrome.

The first job Bob did was to survey the lake carefully. He found it to have an undulating bed varying from deep water with silt pockets to shallow bars with hardly any water covering them. Weed flourished everywhere and the water clarity was excellent. He had kind co-operation from everyone connected with the Aquadrome, so it became possible to plan a campaign and proceed with his 'experiment'.

The water was sounded and the shallows searched extensively for feeding areas. Bob could envisage the fish cruising around in this watery, weedy jungle selecting food from a well-stocked pantry. Because the fish had been brought up on a total diet of natural food any outside alien food would be ignored – the only way to overcome this would be to make the offering tempting and familiar.

Where to fish was another important decision. He needed to anticipate the nature of the fight and allow sufficient room for it, but then again he knew that carp liked cover close by...could he find such a spot?

Eventually, he found one area which seemed perfect, and to make matters a little easier Bob found he could fish from a tiny little island a few yards from the main bank, this being adjacent to the main buildings of the Aquadrome. Time had to be allowed for the groundbait to become effective, and Bob hoped this would happen within a two- to three-week period. However, nothing was left to chance with this experiment.

He made groundbait from a new loaf – all the bread was from the same bakery – and the size of the bait was identical to the ultimate hookbait. This groundbait was spread over a wide area with trails leading back to the actual pitch. The groundbait area was made smaller each day until just before fishing took place. Scent and taste are part of the carp's protective make-up and these were fully allowed for. The same hands moulded the groundbait. Bob also smoked, especially when he fished, so when he made up the groundbait he smoked. He made up the bait at the waterside so the lake's water was always on his hands. By these means he hoped to fool the carp into thinking that the bait was perfectly safe. His

tackle was not overstrong, and the rod was hand-made as was most of Bob's tackle. He used 9lb breaking strain line, and attached to this was a size 2 hook. The landing of the fish was something Bob took a special interest in. He would be alone and with deep water close nothing was left to chance. The landing net problem was solved with the unlikely aid of a bicycle wheel (without spokes), a broom stick and a sack! From this a landing net was born.

The idea for the net was actually suggested by his mother, no less. It worked like this – the fish would be played quite hard, for there were tree stumps nearby, and as the carp weakened it would be brought over the wheel of the landing net and quickly engulfed. As a result, the sack was detached from the bicycle rim and the throat tightly secured with stout cord. All this would happen without the fish even leaving the water! After this was sorted out, all Bob had to do was tie a new sack to the rim of the wheel and he was back in business again!

The only people allowed to night fish during 1957 were Bob and his father, and after carrying out the extensive groundbaiting programme Bob tried the water for a couple of weekends. He had several pick-ups but no fish were hooked. However, as we come to the fateful second weekend in August of that year Bob was about to rewrite the record books...

He arrived late on the Saturday afternoon to find the wind somewhat stronger than of late, and while he set up his tackle on the small island it blew even more. This small island was just that – a tiny mound of 3ft square covered with moss. A couple of small trees also stood precariously balanced on this tiny islet.

It was hardly a night to be out for rain started to fall and, being driven by the wind, it was more than a little uncomfortable. Between the two trees on the island Bob strung up a waterproof canopy in an effort to keep some of the rain off, but it was clear that he was in for a rough night. His father stayed until after midnight then left Bob alone. He returned at 4.30 a.m. wondering if his son had been blown into the lake. But despite the wind and pouring rain, he found Bob

*Bob's record-breaking catches made front-page news.*

more than cheerful! Bob shouted over, 'I've got three fish, Dad.' And what fish they were!

The first came a short while after Bob's father had left. The baiting policy had paid off and this, coupled with the fact that fish were in the general area, ensured that a run or two was likely. After a tense struggle in the teeth of the gale, a big common carp eventually dived into the bicycle rim-cum-landing net. All went well and after he had tied a new hessian sack on to the rim of the wheel Bob cast out again. An hour later, with Bob hanging on grimly to the little trees on the island, his line raced away again. This time an even greater battle ensued and the outcome was uncertain for some time. However, his luck held and a great mirror carp rolled into the net. The same procedure as before soon had the fish safely secured, and after sorting out his tackle he carefully rebaited and cast back into the lake.

He had to wait less than an hour before his bite alarm signalled that another carp had taken the bait. By contrast, this fish fought with hardly a flap of its fins and was soon landed. It turned out to be the largest of the night!

Bob brought the fish ashore and Sam Mackeness rushed around and found some accurate commercial scales. First, the common carp was weighed – it pulled the scales to 24lb 12oz and was a beautifully conditioned and perfectly proportioned fish. The second largest was then weighed – at 27lb 13oz it was a sparsely scaled mirror, again in immaculate condition. Then the largest of the trio came to the scales, this carp looking considerably bigger than the common carp, and so it proved to be. It was a giant of a mirror, all 28lb 4oz of it!

It was the first time in carp fishing history that three such fish had been landed in a single session. After professional pictures were taken all the carp were safely returned to the water and Bob went home for a well-earned rest.

The *Angling Times* of Friday, 16 August 1957 shouted out the headline 'A RECORD CATCH OF HUGE CARP', as they reported this important record-breaking catch of 80lb of carp in a single night! Suddenly Bob Reynolds' name was on everyone's lips and so was that of Billing Aquadrome! The general opinion was that this was indeed an unusual and an outstanding catch, having come from a gravel pit which at the time were considered not capable of growing big fish!

Bob somewhat bathed in the glory of publicity at the time, but hardly had the ink dried on the paper than he was back again at Billing the following Saturday night. In fact, Bob had been at Billing every evening baiting up with large pieces torn from the inside of a new loaf. Again this tactic drew the carp into the baited area just off the little island. Bob cast out after nightfall. The weather, although better than the previous week, did suffer from a fairly coldish wind which refused to die until 4 a.m. Only after all went quiet did Bob get a run, and the by now familiar pattern of playing the fish went into operation. However, this fish really fought and very nearly snagged Bob in some tree roots, but it came ashore with Bob feeling lucky to land it. This fish was a magnificent leather carp with hardly a scale on its huge body.

All lay quiet for some hours. It had just turned daybreak when Bob had yet another run. This fish was the jewel in the crown, for it set a new record for a fully-scaled mirror. Although Redmire had produced a whopper to Jack Opie some years before, Bob's fully-scaled mirror had beaten it by just 4oz! When Bob's two fish were brought to the shore his father and a gathering of well wishers were waiting. The leather carp weighed a mighty 26lb 10oz and the fully-scaled mirror a fantastic 27lb 9oz.

The total weight of his carp haul, taken within a week, was over 135lb. The angling world could hardly believe it, for no angler had caught so many carp over 25lb and no other angler had caught more than one carp over 20lb in a single day. Bob had performed this feat twice in successive weekends! To make Bob's catch even more creditable, all these fish were taken on home-made tackle – a glass-fibre rod, bite indicator and the bicycle rim landing net! By the way, that net was replaced in short order by B. James & Son, the noted makers of the Mk IV carp rod. They produced a lovely split-cane triangular carp landing net to Dick Walker's original design. This was presented by the company for Bob's

*Bob returns the Billing 27lb 9oz fully-scaled mirror, at the time the largest ever caught.*

outstanding catch, but as a bonus Dick Walker, along with Pete Thomas, went to Northampton to deliver the gift personally. Bob used the net extensively in the years to come.

The years between 1957 and 1961 produced little to my knowledge in the way of carp, but it was in the summer of 1961 that Billing once more gave up some of its mighty carp, with many others of lesser proportions.

## THE GATES ARE OPENED

The aquadrome management decided to allow night fishing in 1961 at 7-6d (37p) per rod per night, and many took advantage of it. Johnny Bingham was one who fished hard all summer long, and he was rewarded with several carp up to 24lb. A local angler named Dick Tebbutt caught a lovely 22lb mirror, and dedicated Northampton carp angler Phil Shatford caught four to 17lb. Not to be left out, two noted specimen hunters with a special interest in carp made the long journey up from London to Billing for a number of trips during the summer months. Their names were Bill Keal and Alec Lewis. I knew both of these gentlemen, and indeed in my formative years as a budding specimen hunter I got to know them through the National Association of Specimen Groups, meeting them both at the early conferences that the NASG held in London. Alec and Bill had success during the summer at Billing, catching one each. Bill managed a 9lb common carp, and then a little later Alec struck gold. One night while fishing up by the long islands he had a tremendous run, and after a fight that had Alec gasping at the power of the fish Bill finally put the net under the big carp. Shining the torch on the beast, both agreed that it must weigh over 20lb. They weren't wrong, for Alec's prize was a splendid classical shaped 'Leney' mirror weighing 23lb 13oz.

However, all these captures were somewhat put in the shade by another big carp caught by Bob Reynolds. Bob was a more experienced and wiser carp man by 1961. With the benefit of hindsight he regretted the publicity that he had had in earlier years. People started to watch him closely and fish in the swims after he left, and he was also bombarded with a constant stream of questions. What bait did he use? When was the best time to fish? Was there a record fish swimming in Billing? And so on…

Resigned to the fact that he was not to have the water exclusively to himself any more, Bob studied hard to work out where the carp might be now that as many as half a dozen carp anglers were fishing during most weekends. The knowledge of the water and his confidence in the methods he was using finally meant his line was to lead to a monster carp.

In August 1961, Bob and his friend Pete Andrews tried an area not far from the little island – the scene of his previous success – and on Saturday, 11 August he banked a veritable monster of 33lb 2oz. This thickset mirror was the season's biggest by far, and the fourth largest ever caught!

The *Angling Times* sent a staff photographer up specially on the Sunday morning to get the pictures, and these turned out to be so good as to warrant a centre spread the following week in the paper. They also made great play of the fact that Bob had reported that the carp was caught using banana-flavoured bread paste. A few years later Bob told me the truth – needless to say he didn't

*'33lb 2oz carp with a taste for bananas,' so Bob had us all believe!*

use banana, but it got the people who were hounding him off on a different trail and gave him a little peace and quiet!

The carp he caught was quite possibly one from the original stocking of November 1935 – making it twenty-six years old. However, it is unlikely that this was the best 'grower' from that stocking for Bob had reported sightings of far larger fish. When I met him at Billing in 1970 he told me that during the first season (1957) he saw very big carp on more than one occasion, and during the 1961 season he saw in the back channel (which is just 5yd wide) a fish he thought might weigh 50lb! This was possible as the growing cycle (in terms of bone structure) of the Leney fish had finished, in the Billings case, possibly by 1950, and all the fish had to do was fill out. Although doubt has been expressed in recent years, I tend to agree with Bob on the ultimate size that the Billing fish could reach – a carp approaching 50lb was perfectly possible, I think…

So, 1961 was a highly successful year for carp captures, but it was also the year when the first moves were made to expand and improve Billing Aquadrome as a holiday centre.

## NO SWIMMING AFTER DARK!

Picture the scene: on one side of the lake was a restaurant and dance-hall, a cocktail bar, a small fair, petrol pumps, a swimming pool complete with a neon sign which read 'No swimming after dark', and the entrance to the aquadrome which, naturally, was well illuminated. On two sides of the lake were caravans and on another was a site where campers could pitch their tents. Nearby was another lake where the throaty roar of speed boats could be heard for much of the day. On the carp lake itself, rowing boats were active for most of the daylight hours. A miniature train rumbled around the lake, often until nearly dusk and loaded with noisy holidaymakers. To complete this carp fisher's nightmare, there was also a loudspeaker system rigged up in the trees around the lake, which blared forth music until after dark

and a cheery, 'Good morning caravaners and campers,' not long after sunrise! Until midnight the headlights of cars sent out their beams sweeping across the lake as the aquadrome visitors went about their activities on their way to the bar, dance-hall, caravans or tents. The inevitable courting couples were present in profusion in such idyllic surroundings, a constant nuisance and embarrassment to the carp man, quietly sitting near his rods. The decline of Billing as a carp water had begun…

However, a concerted effort in 1962 by noted anglers Fred Wagstaffe, Johnny Bingham, Phil Shatford, Bill Keal and Alec Lewis (Bob Reynolds had virtually given up fishing there) resulted in an all-out effort to repeat the previous year's wonderful results. But the Billing carp were far from impressed – they proved to be cautious in the extreme that year, and even though much carp fishing was practised only *one* carp was caught all year long, a 14lb mirror which fell to Fred Wagstaffe's rod.

The Saturday night dances had become popular features with visitors to the aquadrome and it was felt that this combined effect and other attractions had made the carp far more wary. Prebaited swims produced nothing more than the dreaded Billing bream. There were vast shoals of these present and they grew to a decent size – easily big enough to swallow a King Edward potato or a fist-sized ball of paste!

Prior to the opening of the 1963 season, Fred, Phil and Johnny Bingham conducted a close study of the lake; gripped with carp fever they were more determined than ever before. They decided on a two-fold plan, picking two areas of the lake and prebaiting heavily with potatoes for a period of some two months. However, as the bream took these baits with such monotonous regularity it slowly became obvious to them that this tactic was wrong. Fred caught the only carp from this prebaited area, and he caught it on floating crust! It was a 9lb mirror. In another area of the lake Bill Keal and Fred caught one each, and they weighed 8lb and 9lb. These fish were taken using bread paste presented on a shallow gravel bar.

*Phil Shatford's determined effort finally produces one of Billing's big carp –
a 32lb common!*

By 1964 Fred Wagstaffe and Phil Shatford really had the bit between their teeth, and deserting any form of prebaiting maintained a constant watch on the lake and fished swims where carp activity had been observed. Success came as a result of this observation, for they noticed a gathering of carp in one corner for several nights. Naturally they fished there. In darkness it was found that the carp fed in among the accumulation of scum which had drifted there on the strong south-westerly wind. They tried floating crust, but to no avail. Then they tried a different tactic and fished this time from a little island so they could fish the approaches to the accumulated debris.

Shortly after dusk one night a slow run occurred on one of Phil's rods. A terrific battle ensued in the close proximity of the island, but heavy pressure from Phil lasting several minutes had the fish swirling close to the bank – even then the fish showed tremendous power and would not come to the net. Finally a great carp came ashore. Fred hurriedly found a torch and, flashing it on the fish the two men gasped as the immense golden flank of a common carp bucked wildly in the landing net. Soon it was up on the scales, and carefully checking the dial Phil registered a weight of exactly 32lb, a just result for Phil as all his efforts during the previous two seasons had gone unrewarded. This carp turned out to be the largest recorded in England that year and placed Billing amongst the best big carp waters in the country, having now produced two carp over 30lb in weight.

There were more changes taking place at the lake and its surroundings in 1965 as one scheme after another was put into operation in order to attract the holiday crowds. It also saw a new 'recruit' in the shape of Jim Gibbinson. Jim was a very successful carp man and an innovative angler who was into all kinds of things to do with tackle, baits, rigs and winter carp fishing. Thoughts of the challenge of Billing had been stirred initially by Bob Reynolds' captures and then by being a friend of Fred Wagstaffe, and as he moved jobs during 1965 he was lucky to be near Northampton. So, Jim's undoubted skills

were brought to bear at Billing. He joined forces with Fred and Phil – they even hired a chalet on the site so that they could spend even more time there!

However, Jim lasted just one season at the water and vowed never to return again! Jim admitted he was defeated, but not by the carp – Jim had to tolerate more than his temperament would allow. The constant noise, both day and night, the sheer amount of people about and the carnival-type atmosphere all added up to a nightmare for Jim. He fished for that one year but never had a run – not from carp that is, but plenty from the big Billing bream! However, you can't catch monster carp from a water that does not hold them, so it was a point of taking the rough with the smooth. Jim's hopes were kept alive by an incident that took place in the close season, but more of this in a minute. The summer saw only one carp caught, this being to Phil Shatford's rod and which was an 11lb common. The fishing at Billing proved to be more difficult than ever before.

So why did men like these keep up the pressure? Quite simply, in reality Billing held big carp – possibly record carp – and Billing carp were in a class of their own.

Of the many sightings of huge carp over the years, only recently did Jim Gibbinson tell me his story of a never-to-be-forgotten evening when he was out in a boat at Billing. He managed to drift within a couple of yards of a monster and could have touched it with the oar. He saw every scale and every fin ray as, in its anxiety to escape from the boat looming up on it, it turned on its side to cross a shallow sand bar and splashed round the boat in an arc. This carp was of common carp scaling and was easily the biggest carp Jim had ever clapped his eyes on. Jim told me that his lasting impression of that carp was, 'It was *twice* the size of several Billing carp I had seen during the close season.'

The realization of a monster common carp being caught from Billing was in fact to come to fruition during 1966 – indeed the year of 1966 turned into a vintage year for super big carp all over the country .

*Jim Gibbinson fishing Billing during his brief affair with the water during the 1965
season. His camouflage set-up was quite superb.*

## SECOND-LARGEST EVER...

It was in the classic carp month of September in
1966 that a local specialist angler, Ray Clay,
arrived at Billing Aquadrome for the start of his
usual all-night session. After an average of two
all-night trips per week since the opening week of
the season, it was by then all second nature to
him. At 7 p.m. the lake had quietened down, and
as the light faded so too did the breeze which had
rippled the lake throughout the day and the water
became calm. He fished a small gravel bar less
than 20yd from the bank in an area where he'd
often spotted carp. All was calm until the stillness
was interrupted by his bite alarm at around
11 p.m. Picking up the rod and striking hard he
immediately felt the immense power of the fish as

it headed for the middle of the lake with Ray
hanging on as best he could.

Many of these long runs occurred, followed by
several shorter ones. However, all held and Ray
was able to bring the huge fish near enough to
attempt to net it. In this spot the water was so
shallow that he could hardly get the net beneath
the fish. Finally, the huge black shape begrudgingly went over the lip of the net. Despite the
alloy handle of the landing net bending double,
Ray struggled and splashed out of the shallows,
hugging the net and its massive contents up on to
the bank, where they lay side by side, heaving!

Ray later described the fish as follows: 'It must
have been then that I realized that not only was
this the largest fish I have ever caught, but it was
the largest that I had ever seen!'

*Ray Clay holding the second largest carp ever caught in England at the time – 42lb. It proved to be the biggest carp landed in Billing's history, though like Redmire others were seen from time to time that appeared to be larger.*

When morning finally came his first attempts at weighing proved that his 28lb spring balance was hopelessly inadequate. Finally Sam Mackeness weighed the big fish accurately on farm balances and established in front of several witnesses that it weighed 42lb. At the time it was the second-largest carp recorded in the UK.

It was a tremendous common carp, and was possibly the same one that Jim Gibbinson had seen in the close season of that year and one that Phil Shatford had reported as witnessing a few years before. Bob Reynolds was little surprised by the news, saying, 'It's still not the largest fish in Billing,' and adding, 'there is at least one, I promise you, a mirror carp that is bigger.'

After this tumultuous event all went quiet at Billing for the next few years, with little being reported in the way of big carp. Most people believed Billing carp were far too hard a proposition, even though the water had produced a string of big fish during the previous ten years. In the mid-1960s, big carp still had an almost 'uncatchable' tag to them, and even though many people tried, few ever succeeded!

The mid-1960s also saw the birth of the specimen hunter – young, eager men with a resolve to outwit the largest fish swimming with new techniques, baits and tackle. Bait certainly had come along in leaps and bounds, and gone were bread paste, lobworms, potatoes and the like. This was the period of the 'special' sausagemeat mixed with rusk; tinned cat food with flour moulded into firm paste. These highly attractive ingredients were scoring with carp all over the country. Waters that seemed impossible to fish for large carp effectively became the target as these methods started to unravel the secrets of catching the monster carp of dreams.

I had a brief flirtation with Billing myself at this time, and it came about through my being a member of the British Carp Study Group, for in early May 1970 the Annual General Meeting of the group was arranged at Billing Aquadrome. But better still, Bob Reynolds (who was a founder member of this most important group) and a young local carp fanatic by the name of Duncan Kay had arranged through Sam Macke-

ness that the aquadrome be closed to the public from midnight on Friday to late Sunday evening. Many of us young carp men took advantage of this chance to fish the famed water. I remember the weather was far from kind that weekend, but although it may have been uncomfortable to fish the conditions for catching a carp were good.

On arrival we were given an introductory document explaining the weekend's arrangements and *A Guide to Billing Aquadrome*, which read as follows:

'Billing Aquadrome contains six lakes, four of which are able to be fished during the normal close season, although it has its own close season from October 1st until March 27th. All the lakes contain carp to a certain extent, the most important of which is the Willow Tree Lake. This lake is extremely hard to fish for carp as there are few carp in it, and there are a large number of medium and big bream which will take anything from a "King Edward" to a "pinky". There are also a large number of holidaymakers' caravans around the banks.

'However, when a fish is caught it is usually worth all the frustration and effort.

'Bob Reynolds has supplied an accurate map. Deep water can be found on the bank downwards from Ray Clay's point towards the bar, and also in the bay near the overhanging trees, where it is six to seven feet deep.

'The lake undoubtedly contains carp in excess of the present record – 44lb – and Ray Clay's 42-pounder which was returned.

'I have personally seen one carp of around 50 pounds in the area around the back channel. This channel is approximately five yards wide, four feet deep and full of sunken branches, but I am quite sure that this is where the best chance lies at the moment, as later in the season there are more anglers and even during the night the fish are scared out into the open water, beyond the islands. However, this is where the next record carp will come from if I get my way.

*The second weekend in May 1970 was the venue for the British Carp Study Group Fish-In/AGM at Billing (the author fished that weekend).*

# THE BRITISH CARP STUDY GROUP

## ANNUAL GENERAL MEETING 1970

**Please admit the bearer of this paper, who is a member of the BCSG, FREE, to Billing Aquadrome, Northampton, between 6 p.m. on Friday May 8th, and midnight on Sunday, May 10th.**

THE PANEL above is your admission "ticket" to Billing Aquadrome. Please take all this paper with you, and show it at the gate.

THE FORMAL MEETING will take place at 11 a.m. on SUNDAY, MAY 10th, in the DANCE-HALL of the WILLOW TREE BAR.

### AGENDA

1. Election of Officers.

2. Hon. Secretary's Report.

3. Treasurer's Report.

4. Subscriptions.

5. Scientific Officer's Report.

6. N.W. Regional Section Organiser's Report.

7. Any other business.

SOME ADVANTAGES of BCSG Membership:—

#### Cash Advantages

1. Discount of 10% on all tackle and angling accessories —if you spend £10 annually, you SAVE £1.

2. Discount on Irish fishing holidays through our member in Ireland.

3. Fishing weekend at Billing Aquadrome, FREE; if you fish, you SAVE AT LEAST £1 10s.

#### Other Advantages

4. Preference for membership of syndicates to fish REDMIRE, ASHLEA POOL, and WADHURST LAKE. We are negotiating with other syndicates for preferential treatment for BCSG members.

5. Free receipt of "THE CARP", official magazine and newsletter of the BCSG, containing news of most of the happenings in the world of carp fishing, and including articles by many of the top names in angling, annual list of all carp taken by members over 10lb., and many other useful features. Published quarterly, and surely well worth *£1 a year* to any carp angler, yet FREE to our members!

6. The chance to see yourself in print. *Your* ideas and experiences can be made known to others through the columns of *our* magazine.

7. A list of names and addresses of members in 26 counties and three countries, which gives BCSG members a carp fishing friend wherever they go!

8. National representation and publicity through the angling press, shows and conferences.

9. The FREE services of biologist Jim Gregory for help with scientific and fishery management problems involving the waters you fish.

10. The opportunity to help carp anglers less experienced and knowledgeable than yourselves, through our Carp Anglers' Advisory Service.

11. Participation in reporting schemes, and other group activities connected with the collection of information about carp and carp fishing, with a view to the future publication of a group book, to which *you* will have contributed.

12. And the unique right to be a member of the BCSG, but to take part in none of the group's activities if you wish, without being thought the less of by your fellow members!

TAKE THE ABOVE NOTES TO THE MEETING, and remember all these advantages when you are asked to vote on an increased subscription! You could pay a sub. of more than £2 a year, and still be in pocket!

'Evening carp fishing is almost useless, night fishing is quite good, but dawn presents the best chance.

'If anyone wishes to fish from one of the islands, waterborne transport has been arranged, free of charge, otherwise boats may be hired from the Aquadrome at 10s (50p) a night.

'*Last Word:*

For floating crust addicts it is well to note that the ducks like it better than the carp do – and there are more of them!'

### Bob Reynolds and Duncan Kay

Alas, no fish were banked that weekend but two people had runs and one carp it seems was hooked.

This was the first time I had met Bob Reynolds. At first he seemed a relaxed and almost flippant kind of bloke, but soon his smiling eyes and wicked sense of humour won us over. He had the look of carp about him, if that's the right expression to use. After a while I could understand why he had caught these fabulous carp. He was simply cleverer than they were!

*The Chris Ball bivvy, set up on one of Billing's islands during the BCSG weekend of 1970. Note the three rods.*

That weekend had the effect of making some carp anglers from the BCSG try again at Billing during that coming season. One such angler was Alf Engers from London, a world champion cyclist who was also at that time a carp fanatic. He made a good many trips up to Billing that year and was rewarded with two carp, although he hooked several more. The two he landed weighed 9lb and 16lb. Small fry I hear you say – but they were Billing carp, and that made all the difference.

It was the local carp anglers who really scored that year. I say local, but in reality it was just two gentlemen: Duncan Kay, who is still a major force in carp fishing these days; and Peter Chillingsworth, again who is still involved in specimen angling. Duncan had known Bob Reynolds for a while and had also found out much himself about the lake and its occupants. His constant determination and observation led his line to a 20lb 8oz mirror during the summer, a real event for young Duncan and one that gave him front cover status of the British Carp Study Group magazine – quite something!

In Peter Chillingsworth's case, here was an angler who could catch any fish – in fact, he was an all-rounder with a number of big fish under his belt – and now he thought was the time for a big carp. Billing was in his locality which made baiting up a practical proposition, and he went about his fishing with guile and patience not unlike Bob Reynolds had done a score years before. When his line raced away into the early evening light he knew it was going to be something special . . . half an hour later he had it in the net, and he knew it had to be a whopper by the gut-wrenching fight it had given.

Fumbling around in his pocket for a torch, its tiny light beam revealed a massive bulk in the landing net. He sorted out the scales but they went down to the limit – and with a big bang. Parting the net he viewed his prize, was it a record breaker? Had he caught the grandfather of all carp? Such are the thoughts that go through

*Billing map from the British Carp Study Group Annual General Meeting documentation of 1970 – drawn by the author from a sketch by Bob Reynolds.*

# BILLING AQUADROME (16 ACRES)

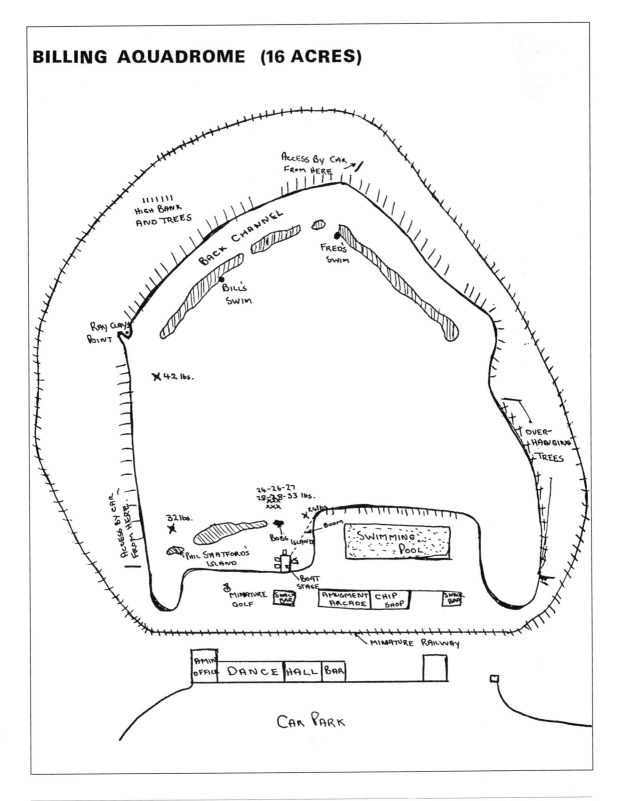

*Duncan Kay made the front cover of the BCSG magazine with his 20lb 8oz mirror caught in 1970.*

your mind when you look at a huge carp in a tiny circle of light.

The rest of the story has a bizarre twist to it for the weighing procedure was somewhat unusual. Peter, faced with a monster carp in the keepsack and not wanting to keep the fish any longer than was absolutely necessary, took the decision to weigh the carp on the aquadrome's gents' toilet scales. I'm sure these were not as accurate as Peter would have liked, for pictures published at the time showed a fish of considerable size and one that looked several pounds heavier than the recorded weight. It's my bet that this fish was one and the same as Ray Clay's of four years previous…exciting isn't it!

## MODERN TIMES

We have to come forward a long way in time before a Billing carp was next reported. There are gaps in the information, but investigations have been made and they show that more than a dozen years elapsed before a notable carp was again reported from Billing. I know this sounds incredible, but there are reasons for it. One was the fact that in the Northampton area an explosion of good carp waters had come of age and offered carp anglers some super fishing. Also, huge carp were being caught from lots of other parts of the country. Billing's holiday atmosphere was more popular than ever: the banks and islands were stripped of vegetation, boats infested the water by day and a noisy disco blasted long into the night. It's little wonder that few tried their hand at carp fishing in these surroundings.

However, enter on the scene one sixteen-year-old fisherman named Simon Faulkner, armed with a lobworm as bait and a 4lb line intended for tench – the result? A lovely shaped mirror which weighed 26lb 4oz. In 1985 it was an usual event, for almost all carp fisherman had forgotten about Billing in the passing of time. Of course, there were carp anglers fishing at Billing, although no fish of notable size were reported for over ten years!

In 1988 two local specialist anglers started a campaign to ascertain whether Billing had any surprises left. Their names were Mark Harrison and Russ Labrum, and from mid-July 1988 until March 1989 they spent over 1,100 hours each at the Willow Tree Lake. Not all this time was spent fishing though, because during the summer and autumn daylight fishing was out of the question as the ducks were diving constantly for the baits. However, the daylight hours were spent observing the fish and generally surveying the lake's contours; this considerable knowledge gave them a good insight into the carp's habits as well. They saw several very good carp and some lesser ones, the bigger fish presenting a challenge that only a dedicated approach could hope to get near. They implemented a heavy baiting campaign, and although the ducks would gang up and descend on these areas, sometimes the only baits the ducks could find were their hookbaits so they knew that the carp were eating the loose feed.

In the first week of September success came to Russ when at 3 a.m. he had a run to one of his rods. After a strong tussle a tremendous 33lb 3oz mirror was safely netted – a marvellous achievement, and although it was never reported nationally everyone toasted his health in the local area, and why not?

This was only the fifth carp ever from the venue that bettered 30lb. A few weeks later Russ caught a 13lb 4oz mirror, a young looking fish that bore no resemblance to the original Billing fish. Russ thought that somehow it must have found its way into the lake by other means. Later, during one afternoon towards the end of October, he found a good fish rolling in a corner of the lake. Keeping the ducks occupied with some dog biscuits, he cast to the fish and within thirty minutes he had a glorious run. At the end of his line was a 23lb 4oz mirror, which when he checked the press cuttings, proved to be the same fish which Simon Faulkner had landed at 26lb 4oz in 1985.

Winter approached and the aquadrome closed, but Mark and Russ were given permission to continue fishing. On the only morning that snow fell Russ caught a 16lb 8oz common carp. This fish had been caught a month earlier at 17lb by a friend, Dave Luck. Although Russ and Mark were to receive no further action, they were well pleased with their results.

*Russ Labrum shows off his 33lb 3oz Billing mirror – after close study it dawned on the author that it was the same carp that Bob Reynolds had caught in 1961!*

At the start of the 1989 season Mark resumed his determined approach to the water, and this included many nights sitting quietly by his rods waiting for the big fish to bite. The aquadrome was busy as usual, but Mark put all this behind him, such is the pull of big carp. He didn't have to wait long, for in July his line finally led to a monster. The awe-inspiring thought of a big 'Leney' Billing carp came true for Mark in the shape of a 36lb mirror. This was more than a just reward for Mark, who showed that through sheer effort and plain good angling he could come up with the goods.

Having talked to both the gentlemen concerned it is interesting to note their conclusions as to the present fish stocks. They spent many hours of observing the lake and exploring every area of it in gin-clear water (they were often able to drift above the carp without even disturbing them). Their opinion is that the lake now contains a very small head of carp – no more than ten with almost definitely only two or maybe three of the original mirrors left.

Apart from the thirty- and the twenty-pounders already caught, they think there is another fish around the 25lb mark. Then they think there are just two common carp of around 17lb, a few low-double-figure mirrors and some smaller common carp – there is, of course, the possibility that some fish may have eluded their eyes.

Maybe someone, some day will land an unknown fish – I hope so.

As I write in autumn 1992, just like Redmire, Billing still keeps going...but what of the carp themselves? Well, I believe at least two of the original 1935/6/7 fish are still swimming around in its waters. They, the sole lasting survivors, are the end of the 'Leney' strain at Billing and are now coming up to the ripe old age of sixty! These grand old fish have seen all before them through the years and although they may have been hooked a few times, they have evaded capture until only very recently – or so I thought!

Late one evening I was here at home in my Carproom and was looking through the pictures

*Simon White landed Bob Reynolds' big mirror again in the autumn of 1992, thirty-one years on from its first capture – could it be the only survivor from the original stocking of November 1935?*

Russ and Mark had sent me when it suddenly clicked that the fish they had caught recently – the 30lb mirror – looked familiar. After checking, it dawned on me that it was one and the same fish that Bob Reynolds had caught way back in 1961! When Russ caught it in 1988, some twenty-seven years later it had altered in weight by only one single ounce!

More detective work revealed that the 23lb 4oz fish that Russ landed was the same as Duncan Kay's one caught in the BCSG year of 1970. Even more recently, just as the book was nearly finished, I spotted in the angling press a report of a 37lb 4oz mirror from Billing. The picture that appeared confirmed this grand old warrior as the same thirty-pounder that Bob Reynolds, Mark Harrison and Russ Labrum had caught previously.

Like most big carp throughout the country, there seems to be a growth factor that is unprecedented during these last few years, and without doubt they all appear to be getting a lot bigger! Simon White, the angler who landed this fish, tells me that it is known as Samson. This is a just name for this strong carp that is approaching its sixtieth year.

Sadly, the monsters spotted in Bob Reynolds' era are no longer seen – unless, that is, you know different...!

# 5 THE ELECTRICITY CUT – BIG RIVER CARP

*Warm water and cold carp.*

## INITIAL STOCKING

Recently I had an opportunity to view a vast carp in a case, at the owner's home. He is the proprietor of one of the largest independent tackle manufacturing companies in Britain. I told him that the last time I had seen this cased carp was back in the late 1960s at the National Angling Show, which that year was staged at the Royal Horticultural Halls at Westminster in London. It was centre stage on the *Angling Times* stand and drew a big audience for most of the day. So why the excitement? Well, it was the largest carp to be caught from a river in England. And not the Thames, the Trent, the Severn or the Avon, but

from a tiny stretch of water off the main River Nene at Peterborough. The unlikely name of this carp fisher's paradise? The Electricity Cut!

The new National River Carp Record caught from the 'Cut' was a gloriously shaped mirror weighing 34lb 4oz. This carp topped an amazing string of captures from this small reach of water that had gained almost cult status within carp fishing circles for more than a decade. Although it's fair to say that carp had been caught from rivers far and wide, their pursuit was largely ignored by carp fishers as a very big carp coming from a river was almost unheard of.

The restocking of the UK's waters after World War II was slow to start with – indeed, The Surrey Trout Farm records show comparatively few orders for 'kings' leaving their depots in the

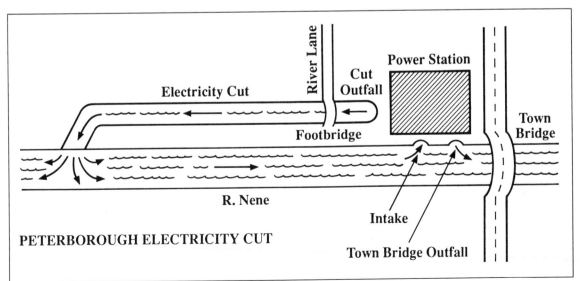

*Map of Peterborough's Electricity Cut showing the power station and its warm-water influence, a key factor that made the Cut such an important venue.*

years 1945–50. However, come the 1950s things started to change. One consignment recorded was in March 1952. This order, for 5,000 yearling carp, was purchased by the Nene and Welland Fishery Board who controlled the Nene catchment area. These fish were destined for a whole variety of waters in the area, but we know that over 1,500 were released at various points along the River Nene. Of these, several hundred were placed in the river not far from Peterborough. One can only speculate as to their movements in the years that followed.

After this stocking there were recorded instances of match anglers fishing in the area being broken by large fish, although this could have come about by fish other than carp. The potential size these carp could reach and their numbers were not realized until the turn of 1959 when a big carp was landed from the Cut itself. It fell to Don Barnes, a Peterborough angler who used a 4lb line and bread paste in the hope of some bream. With such light tackle a forty-five minute battle ensued, with the carp careering up and down the Cut in a seemingly uncontrollable fashion. Eventually, and with help from a nearby angler, he bundled the fish into a small landing net. It turned out to be a 20lb 6oz mirror and was the first carp weighing over 20lb recorded from the Cut.

Late in 1960 another report appeared in the press:

'Fishing the middle of the river with cheese paste intended for chub, local angler Wilfred Richardson hooked a carp in spite of two motor boats passing by seconds before, and in spite of a group of children swimming and splashing a few yards to the left of the angler. This capture came where the Nene was joined by the Electricity Cut. Wilfred had arrived at River Lane at 3.30 p.m. and took the 14 pounder half an hour later, on just his second cast! It fought well against heavy tackle for 10 minutes before being netted by Albert Nightingale. This was the first carp Mr Richardson had taken from the river itself, however he had landed several from the Electricity Cut, including a 12lb mirror.'

These recorded instances are some of the first that give us an idea to the potential of the Cut itself.

It was easy to see why the Cut was an area that the carp so liked. The quarter-mile-long Cut was, in fact, an artificial canal dug for the specific purpose of discharging the artificially warmed water from Peterborough's power station into the River Nene. The accompanying diagram shows what the Cut's topography was like: rather uninteresting and quite uniform in depth. There was not much in the way of cover and it was far removed from what a carp fisher would call a nice quiet venue! In summer, when the flow rate of the river was negligible, the water from the Town Bridge outfall tended to recirculate back towards the station's intake grills, causing difficulties in the power station's cooling system. Therefore, water was discharged into the Cut where it cooled somewhat before reaching the river. It was in winter that this area attracted the carp, for the Cut was used primarily to prevent the river icing over.

Although not in use all the time, anglers could find the power station generating electricity any time between 7 a.m. and 11.30 p.m. The push of water that could come down the Cut was amazing, and Jim Gibbinson once stated it could be something between 1 or 2 million gallons per hour! Even in the depths of winter, you could at times record a temperature around 60°F in the Cut, and it was this warm water that attracted the carp like a magnet.

Naturally, the water at the end nearest the outfall itself was considerably warmer than that at the far end where it entered the main river, but this was not always the case. Jim Gibbinson told me once: 'Fred Wagstaffe and I arrived one time on a winter's evening to find the Cut not being used. But it had been used earlier and had retained its warmth quite well.' Jim recorded a temperature of 60°F at the footbridge by the outfall. Then the Cut started to flow again as the power station began generating, but as the generators had not had time to warm up cold water was entering the Cut. In effect, this cold water had gradually pushed the warm water out of the

Cut! Within an hour, however, Jim had recorded the Cut's water temperature in the fifties and rising. This kind of temperature change must have played havoc with the carp – imagine the fish all nicely comfortable in a water temperature of around 60°F when within fifteen minutes or so they are surrounded by considerably colder water. They could move ahead of the flow where the water was still warm, but the further they moved the cooler the water became. Within an hour the carp wouldn't be able to find any water as warm as before, so back up against the flow they would have to travel – only to find lovely warm water again! Of course, this supposition may be entirely wrong, but do consider it.

The river held plenty of food for the carp grew well, and as we have seen double-figure fish were starting to show. However, it was through plea-sure anglers fishing the Cut in winter and being continually smashed up that word soon got around. The popular opinion was that the culprits responsible were carp!

## A POPULATION OF GREAT CARP

As word got out anglers started to appear on the banks of the Cut armed with more substantial tackle and using baits like potato and large balls of paste. Come September 1961, the weather and water were beginning to get somewhat cooler and the carp started to enter the Cut's warmer waters so that they could thrive through the winter months.

It seems that many spent most, if not all, of the winter in and around the Cut. Just how many of

*Peter Nisbet with an early Cut fish of 21lb 5oz – it was destined to become the Cut's most famous inhabitant!*

the 'Leney' carp spent their time in the Cut we can only guess, but it was a considerable number. By 1967 at least forty-one carp were reported, all weighing over 20lb in weight (including repeat captures), with half a dozen recorded as topping the 30lb mark!

Back to September 1961 and the second of the Cut's big carp was reported. It commanded headline status in *Angling Times* and a big picture accompanied the news story. This super-looking carp weighed in at 21lb 5oz, was landed by Wroxham schoolteacher Peter Nisbet and was to become a famous inhabitant as we follow the Electricity Cut fish through the years. Other double-figure carp were also caught throughout that winter but it was to be the following November before the next big Cut carp was landed. This fish, a mirror, weighed 22lb and angler Paul Hall had tricked the fish into picking up a ball of cheese paste.

In the warmer months the carp did move out back into the main river and a 20lb 8oz mirror was caught by Mr Buck in June 1962. I have since discovered that this carp is the same fish as was caught from the main river the previous September by local Peterborough angler Ted Hill. Using light tackle and paste as bait to land

the 20lb fish, Ted reported, 'I think I was more tired than the fish when I finally landed it.' Exciting stuff!

The following two winters saw more big Cut carp on the bank as good carp anglers started to fish the water. One of the regulars at this stage was Fred Wagstaffe who, although still heavily involved at Billing Aquadrome during the summer months (*see* Chapter 4), found the winter pursuit of warm-water carp a great opportunity. After several close encounters he finally put one on the bank. This carp was caught almost at the point of the outfall itself, right where the rough water tumbled in – often an area favoured by the carp. Fred chose to ledger with a potato, and as the fish weighed 24lb it proved to be a personal best for Fred at the time.

The most popular method for fishing the Cut at the time was to fish a potato or paste bait just over the marginal ledge, the bait usually being dropped in the margins under the rod tip and the current allowed to bring it neatly into position up against the ledge.

Many people who were fishing the Cut at the same time said it was only a matter of time before a 30lb carp would be caught, and so it proved to be. It would be the first Leney 30lb carp caught

*Phillip Buck with a 20lb 8oz carp from the main river at Orton, near Peterborough. This, along with Ted Hill's twenty-pounder from the North Bank, showed that not all the carp lived around the Cut area.*

from a river in England, and the capture caused quite a stir at the time. Following is the story.

The captor was Stan Hill of Grantham who was a member of the local specimen group. Along with his friends Bernard and Dave Goodrum, he often fished at the Cut. It was a weekend at the end of October in 1964 that all three arranged another trip to the famous fishery. Arriving on the Friday evening they decided to do a little exploratory work with a thermometer before choosing where to fish. This revealed a temperature of 66°F at the outflow and 58°F at the far end where it empties into the river. Assessing the situation, Bernard and Stan decided to fish a spot roughly half-way along the Cut in the vicinity of the 'Bush' swims. By contrast, Dave Goodrum fished not far from the point where the Cut joined with the Nene, and Fred tried again near the outflow in the swirling, moving water.

As night advanced everything became still. The incredible sweet, sickly scent from the nearby sugar-beet factory hung in the air, and the rhythmic distant sound of the trains as they clattered over the bridge a few hundred yards away were the only things noticeable. Steam and mist would often rise off the hot water as the cold winter's night progressed. On the bank the rats kept you alert – the Cut could boast more rats than most carp waters.

The coldness of the October night was broken when at 2 a.m. Stan's bite alarm burst into life. A quick strike resulted in a hollow feeling for Stan as the fish had already slipped the hook. Recasting, Stan told the tale to Bernard who had come along the bank to see what had happened. As the two men talked, Stan's bite alarm again came to life – he had another run! There was no mistake this time as Stan's answering strike was met with a substantial solid resistance. Straight away, the fish ripped off 30yd from the reel, then heavy pressure resulted in the fish turning. It bored heavily, creating a huge swirl that both men saw clearly through the blackness of the night. Suddenly the carp doubled back on itself, moving quickly past Stan and going another 20yd or so in the other direction. Then sidestrain turned the

fish as Stan slowly started to exercise some control.

At this stage Bernard was crouching by the water's edge with the big net already waiting. The fight was far from over, however, as the fish plunged strongly on a short line near the marginal weeds. In a flurry it was in the net first time. The coldness was suddenly forgotten as Bernard and Stan struggled up the steep, slippery slopes of the bank. Eventually both men staggered up on to flat ground. They had made it!

The mesh of the huge net was parted to reveal the prize, and the tiny beam of torchlight shone on a massive mirror carp. With frost starting to form they transferred the carp quickly to the sack and secured it in the margins.

When daylight came Fred Wagstaffe drove into Peterborough and soon Russell Hole and some colleagues from the *Angling Times* arrived on the bank. The carp was weighed accurately at 31lb 12oz, was photographed and was then subsequently returned to the water.

I once wrote to Russell Hole years ago to ask for a particular picture I'd seen reproduced of Stan Hill's thirty-pounder, and he wrote back asking why I wanted one. I told him that it was just a superb picture of a very big carp. He very kindly sent me a whole plate black and white photograph. Sadly, I would have loved you to see it as well, but uncharacteristically for me I've lost it!

## THE PRESSURE STARTS

Two months after Stan Hill's catch, and with the weather even colder, a young Peterborough angler named Peter Harvey who was just sixteen years old was fishing in the Cut with potato. Just as it was getting dark a sizzling run came to his bait. To his credit, Peter handled the fight with considerable skill and eventually landed a monster 33lb 12oz mirror carp. Another new National River Carp Record!

Then, just after the turn of the year London angler Peter Hemingway (after some close misses with Cut carp) finally put a whopper on the

*Sixteen-year-old Peter Harvey, who would often cycle to the river, caught the new river carp record in freezing conditions. It was Peter Nisbet's 21-pounder of just three years before, but it now weighed 33lb 12oz!*

bank. Peter was one of a number of carp anglers hailing from the south of England, for the Cut's fame had spread far and wide with interest from all over the country. This carp equalled the new National River Carp Record of 33lb 12oz, but more than that, it was the same fish! It had fallen for a potato bait twice in two months! This carp became quite famous (as did Peter Hemingway) as for a time it was used in advertisements for Davenport and Fordham, a major rod manufacturer at the time, while they promoted their widely used hollow-glass Farstrike carp rod.

Shortly afterwards, an angler who had become synonymous with the Electricity Cut caught his first twenty-pounder from the water. His name was Dave Goodrum. If you mention the Cut to Dave you will realize that to him it is far more than a characterless piece of water. He knew the place better than most, and its moods and atmosphere were special to Dave. The cold winter nights when runs were few and far between did nothing to dampen Dave's enthusiasm.

In early January 1965 Dave Goodrum again went to the Cut. It was bitterly cold with a heavy frost already starting to form as he arranged the tackle and settled down under a mountain of blankets and waterproof gear! The anglers who fished through the winter at night on the banks of

the Cut had none of the refinements we modern carp men have, such as moon boots and warm, quilted one-piece suits. Look at the pictures of the day and you will see tank suits, great thick jumpers and parka coats, long cotton or canvas padded coats. The harshness of the weather was put to one side, however, as the pull of big carp was stronger!

Dave Goodrum remembers the night of 2 January only too well.

'As I walked along the bank with my burden of gear I noticed that the steam from the water was very thick. The smoke from the sugar-beet factory came drifting down the bank, giving the air around a sweet, sickly smell; after a few winters down the Cut you'd get used to it.

'I arrived at my pitch and dumped the gear with a great sigh of relief. Although it was a very cold night I was sweating quite hard. After a short rest, a cigarette and a cup of tea I started to tackle up. I was using two Mk IV carp rods and Mitchell reels, hooks were size 2 tied direct to the line. When everything was arranged I threw a few potatoes in for groundbait. I checked the temperature of the water – it was 68°F, not bad at all.

'I baited one rod with a small potato and cast it about 3yd out. The other rod was baited with

*London angler Peter Hemingway travelled to the Cut in February 1965 and equalled the river carp record. The similarity didn't end there either – it was with the same fish!*

a large ball of paste, and this was cast to the centre of the Cut. The net was then set up and all the bait placed out of reach of the rats. With everything arranged to my satisfaction I settled down for the night. I sat there in the misty darkness, alert for any sound that meant carp! As I looked down the bank I could see that Stan Hill was still setting up. The ground looked whiter now as the frost became harder. I heard the 'plop' of Stan's bait as it hit the water and the buzzing of his bite alarm as he fiddled with it.

'I had a glance at my clock – it was 11.35 p.m. I knew that the Cut would stop flowing shortly as the power station shut down for the night.

'The hours passed slowly by – I think that it was about 4 a.m. when the buzzer on my right-hand rod stuttered and came to life. It was the potato rod. I checked that the line was running out – it was. I picked up the rod, slammed in the bail arm and struck. I connected. The rod bent over in an exciting curve, the clutch of the reel screamed! A heavy and powerful fish tore up the

*Dave Goodrum was an angler who knew the Electricity Cut better than most. Here he is with his first twenty-pounder from the river – an immaculate Leney mirror weighing 24lb. Dave's account of the fishing at the country's top river water gives us an insight into the endurance necessary in very cold conditions.*

Cut to my left. This fish could really pull. After the fish had gone 50yd it turned and came back at me with alarming speed. I had to wind very fast to keep in contact with it. Just as the fish was about level with me it shot in towards the bank, crashed through a small bed of marginal weeds then ran out into the main channel again! The manoeuvre had me worried, the line had somehow contrived to get caught round the roots of the reeds – I could not free it – and the fish was still taking line. I expected the line to part at any moment…but it held.

'I called Stan and quickly explained the situation to him. The fish stopped taking line. Stan was soon in the water, hands groping among the reed roots…soon he had it free. I got the rod tip up and wound furiously; I prayed that the fish was still on. The line shot tight as the fish produced a savage wrench on the rod, and it rolled heavily on the surface some 30yd down the bank. I walked down towards the fish and soon had it on a short line. By now I was near the small footbridge that spans the Cut. The inevitable happened – the reel screamed and the fish shot under the bridge putting the line dangerously close to the concrete support. I put the rod over nearly horizontal to the water. I had to keep the line away from the supports. The pressure told and I managed to ease the carp gently back to my side of the bridge – I wanted him as far away from the bridge as possible.

'At this stage of the battle the carp had been on about thirty-five minutes, a long while, yet it was another fifteen minutes at least before I felt him begin to tire. The fish circled in front of me, boring deep and doggedly. Stan knew that the end was near and was crouching with the net. The fish broke surface some five yards out. Gingerly I coaxed him over the net. I put the rod down with a sigh of relief, my arm was just about numb!

'"It's a twenty," Stan said, adding, "Well done Dave."

'At that stage I remember getting the shakes; I lit a cigarette to calm my nerves. We put the carp in the big sack and made it safe. Stan gave me a cup of tea and also his congratulations. As I stood there on the banks of the Cut I had a tremendous feeling of satisfaction; I had at last caught my first twenty-plus carp!

'In the morning we weighed and photographed the fish. It weighed 24lb exactly.'

So ends Dave Goodrum's exciting story of a big Cut carp. In 1965 a 24lb carp from a river was a very big fish indeed. This carp was a perfect Leney mirror displaying a big length, large fins and beautiful scaling, and most important of all it was well deserved.

Within a year Dave Goodrum had unlocked the key to the Cut for he landed three more big fish, the first coming in October. This one was caught on a potato again and weighed 21lb 4oz. Then in December 1965 he captured the most perfect common carp ever – look at the picture reproduced on page 118 and you will see what I mean.

The following February of 1966, during another night of extreme freezing conditions, Dave found that hot water from the power station had been pouring in hour after hour. This had encouraged one or two carp to investigate the floating crusts Dave had introduced after dark, and soon after he cast a crust close to where the carp had showed to the loose feed. He was spot on, for within a minute the large crust disappeared in a heavy swirl. It was obvious that Dave had hooked another big carp and one that was not happy at all! It shot off a long way up the Cut causing Dave all kinds of problems – that bridge again! But after the first long run Dave was able to control the carp much better than previous big ones he'd hooked. In short order it was in the net, and as if by some strange coincidence this carp, which had fought the least of the three big Cut carp Dave had captured, was the largest! It was a super 25lb mirror.

By the mid 1960s carp anglers were not content with fishing the Cut just through the winter months. Their baiting campaigns took into account the fact that the carp, although spending most of the summer months in the main river, were never far from the Cut at this time and even came into it on occasions.

## A RECORD-BREAKING YEAR

The dawning of the 1965 season saw a collection of anglers ready for the start of the new season. Among them was a 21-year-old-Polish angler from Neasden in London, his name being

William Beta. Quite how he came to be fishing the Cut at the start of the season is something I've never been able to find out. Indeed, as the story unfolds we will find that carp fishing ran in the family, for his mother Ilona was also to appear on the banks of the Cut before the year was out! However, back to 16 June.

Young William had cast out a cheese bait in an attempt to entice a Cut carp. The resulting run proved that Cut carp did indeed have a liking for cheese. The battle – which was watched by a gathering of well-wishers – was full of drama as the carp careered up and down the Cut, making other anglers withdraw their lines as the big fish would have become caught in them. It was a good fight but one from which William emerged the champion. In front of a crowd of people (who cheered when the fish was beaten) William care-

*Hungarian-born William Beta was just twenty-one years old when he broke the river carp record with this 34lb 4oz mirror from the Cut. The big mirror proved again to be the same fish as Peter Nisbet's from September 1961. This carp broke its own record on no less than six occasions in four years!*

fully and skilfully guided the carp towards the net. Straight away William knew this was a very big carp – a fish with a tremendous girth besides its length. On the scales it went, and its weight was accurately recorded at 34lb 4oz. It was then placed in a sack to recover and the *Angling Times* was contacted. Some time later the *Angling Times* crew duly came, but as the sack was parted so a disaster was realized – the fish had died.

Whether the sack caused the fish's death or not is hard to judge, but the fact remained that it had perished. To comfort William Beta, the *Angling Times* offered to have the carp set up. The cost of this – even in 1965 – was considerable, and naturally William was more than happy to accept this offer, some solace for the tragedy.

Now, years later and with the benefit of hindsight we know this carp to be a well-known River Nene inhabitant. First caught back in September 1961 by Peter Nisbet, afterwards it was to appear on the bank another four times before William Beta landed the beauty.

When young William returned home he was the toast of the street – not surprisingly really as he was the new record river carp holder. His mother Ilona, who also was an angler, discussed the validity of visiting the famous Cut herself to fish for the carp. William no doubt explained all he knew as to the tactics, bait and location needed. Ilona went to the water throughout the course of the summer. At a guess, I'd have thought it would have raised a few eyebrows, for after all a lady fishing purposely for carp was somewhat unusual in those days. But fish she did, and in October of that year using paste as bait she mastered a magnificent 25lb mirror carp. Not content with that, the following June found Ilona Beta fishing the Cut again. This time, with nice warm weather, Ilona found the carp taking floating crusts with gusto. A carefully positioned bait was soon taken, and a grand fight then ensued. To Ilona's credit she played and landed the carp without any trouble at all. It was another big fish, a twenty-one-pounder and possibly the first twenty-pounder from the Cut that season!

This mother and son who both caught carp over 20lb in weight marked a first in carp fishing

*Magnificent 23lb common captured by Dave Goodrum in early December 1965 after a night of freezing conditions. The bait used was potato.*

history – the Electricity Cut had turned up another record and the carp world took note…

| | |
|---|---|
| **Elliott Smith** | 26lb |
| **Dave Moore** | 23lb 4oz |
| | 22lb |
| | 20lb 8oz |

## LOCAL BOY MAKES GOOD

Enter on the scene one Elliott Smith, a local fisherman who had become interested in carp during this period. I guess he'd heard the reports of big carp coming from the Electricity Cut and was keen to find out if they were at all true. Another specimen hunter from the area was Dave Moore – he too had become interested in big carp and the Cut's reputation was hard to resist. These two anglers, although coming to the Cut as separate individuals, soon got to know one another. In truth, this kind of fishing and the size of the quarry was something new to them both. Of all the anglers to fish the Cut, it was Elliott who I remember the most – I am still in contact with him these days and he's still totally carp mad!

Elliott hit the jackpot almost straight away with the first big carp he had ever caught; this was on New Year's Day in 1966. The fish weighed a little over 22lb and was one of five twenty-pounders that Elliott and Dave Moore caught in January 1966 alone! The others were as follows:

These kinds of results came from plain good angling as well as being able to withstand the rigorous cold of winter night fishing. Just as others had done before, Dave and Elliott seemed to have that in-built endurance to keep alert and keen in the most severe of weather conditions. Many is the time when the cold chilled their bodies almost to the point of them giving up and going back to their warm homes. But the carp bites were coming in at just the right frequency to make them forget the frosty conditions and concentrate on the exciting prospect of a big Cut carp!

Elliott basked in the glory of the publicity that *Angling Times* gave him at the time and later with the subsequent captures, but soon he realized that publicity meant more anglers which made less bank space for the locals.

He fished hard down at the Cut, catching a good number of carp, some of which were small but many of which large. His fishing consisted of Friday evening to Sunday lunchtime sessions the whole winter through. The baits in use still

*Dave Moore, a very successful Cut angler, with a carp affectionately known as Old Lumpy. It weighed 24lb 8oz when Dave landed it in September 1966.*

generally consisted of bread in one form or other, flake being a particular favourite – although the flow could give problems by washing the bait from the hook, especially when the power station was pumping at full tilt. Also, small fish would be a nuisance by reducing the bait to the size of a pea. Big bream would occasionally make an appearance, sometimes giving the carp angler a heart attack as a fast run would occur. The humble potato also still had many fans and was still catching the carp.

Not long after Elliott Smith started to fish for the Cut carp, there appeared on the banks foreigners. Carp anglers from other areas of the UK had been drawn to the Cut's banks, all intent on catching a twenty-pounder, the fish most carp anglers dream about. They brought with them new baits, and these were called specials. In the main these were the wildly successful pet food mixes of tinned Kit-E-Kat and other cat and dog foods. Another great bait was sausage paste, and these kinds of baits were then mixed with rusk or flour to turn them into a highly attractive and durable paste. The size of bait was unusually pretty big, at least chicken egg size or bigger (the latter were called donkey chokers!).

## The Net Spreads Wider

Much of this development in bait came from the carp anglers of Kent (though some tell me differently), and it was these keen carpers of Kent and the Home Counties that Elliott saw more

*Dave Goodrum prepares to cast a freelined potato into the margins of the Cut. With his brolly only half-covering the angler, and heavy blankets and a waterproof cover being his only protection against the elements, clearly he must have half-frozen to death!*

frequently than he liked. To start with they kept themselves to themselves, but as always when you find a collection of people fishing the same stretch of water for week after week, they obviously got to know one another! The brotherhood of angling soon got to work and Elliott found out what a great bunch of fellows and what good company they were in those 'brass monkey' days.

The Cut gave a number of anglers their first ever twenty-pounder as well as their best ever carp. One such angler was the celebrated Jim Gibbinson who, through his friendship with Fred Wagstaffe and Dave Goodrum, had decided to join them for an attack on the Cut carp during the winter of 1966/7. Jim was very much ahead of his time, a real thinking angler who was willing to try anything and everything! Indeed many of the present-day big fish men read every word Jim had to say on carp and carp fishing in their formative years.

Jim's big moment came in the depths of winter that year when he too found a big carp on the end of his line. A large piece of crust on a short tail used in conjunction with a running lead was the perfect combination for the conditions Jim found – the flow was very fast that day. Although having landed carp to nearly 20lb in the past, this River Nene carp was easily the largest he had ever put on the bank.

Yes, Jim had caught the elusive prize, in his case a 24lb common carp. This was a very well deserved capture, but was one Jim strangely enough did not publicize at the time. The first most people knew of it was when a picture of it appeared in Jim's excellent book, aptly named *Carp* (Macdonald and Company), which was published in 1968!

Another young man from Kent by the name of Grahame Igglesden was making visits around this time too. He was like many of the period: mad keen and sporting the latest in tackle and tactics. With a good many double-figure carp to his name, he wanted a twenty pounder as so many others did. In Grahame's case, however, the event was not quite what he had had in mind.

After fishing through another cold night in a spot roughly half-way along the Cut (incidentally next to Jim Gibbinson), his bait, a piece of flake, was taken by a fish that meant business. It took off at a terrific pace and was able to run a long way down the Cut unabated. The reason? Grahame wasn't by his rods. In truth, he was only a few yards away talking to Jim Gibbinson! It says something of how this was viewed in those days, for Grahame still felt slightly uneasy about the

*Rare picture of Jim Gibbinson's first ever twenty-pounder, a 24lb common caught from the Electricity Cut in March 1966. Strangely, Jim kept this capture under wraps, and it did not come to the public's attention until some time later.*

*Grahame Igglesden was an up-and-coming specimen hunter from south London, who made a few trips to the Cut in early 1966. This 20lb common came in March while he was at the Cut fishing alongside Jim Gibbinson.*

had become legends and had helped produce a unique fishery – one whose fame was to be known the country over. Yet in the midst of this, one thought comes across strongly. Jim Gibbinson once wrote: 'It is ironic that, whereas many waters are lost to the march of industry and "progress", the Cut was actually created by industry. Were it not for the sprawling acres of Peterborough's power station, there would be no Cut...'

For people like Peter Harvey, Peter Hemingway, Dave Moore, Dave Goodrum, Stan Hill, Grahame Igglesden and a host of other anglers whom you might never have heard of, this water was their finest hour. To other anglers, those who are still very much around these days, the Cut represented yet another stepping stone up the carp ladder. But that said, for all these anglers it's ironic that their angling highlight at the time did not come from a quiet, lily-covered pool surrounded by lush open meadows where the only sounds you could hear were waterfowl and carp leaping. Instead it came by a bare, cold stretch of water infested with rats and many other anglers, where night after night was spent often in freezing conditions, almost in the heart of Peterborough – the Electricity Cut.

These days the Cut has no warm water discharged into it whatsoever, for the power station closed down around the mid-1970s, but the River Nene still holds big carp. Reports have persisted over the years since the Electricity Cut's heyday and there can be little doubt that the Nene still does hold very big carp. Besides ones I have mentioned that have been caught within the last ten years, as I write there have been reports of other fish. In September 1992 Gavin Attwell, a carp angler who'd already banked carp of 28lb 6oz and 21lb 5oz, latched into a beautiful, long and perfectly scaled 29lb 4oz common carp. As far as I can make out these captures of Gavin's have come from an area close to where the Cut joins the river. It is possible that some of the fish being caught these days are original fish from the 1952 one-year-old stock, thus making any survivor forty-seven years of age. Is this possible? Well it's a nice thought!

capture of this carp when we talked recently – some twenty-five years later! But that aside, he managed to bring the carp under control, and with Jim Gibbinson holding the landing net he made no mistake when at last the big common carp finally rolled into the net. Grahame's prize weighed 20lb exactly!

Although the Electricity Cut continued to produce odd big carp in the latter half of the 1960s, the pumping of warm water was by then often erratic, which meant that the fish didn't feed with their previous gusto and were spending less time in the Cut. However, by this time Elliott Smith (now Symak) had created a record seven twenty-pounders landed by one person. It is a record that he will hold forever, I suppose, for by the time the Americans had landed on the moon, the days of Britain's top warm-water fishery were numbered.

William Beta's 34lb 4oz mirror has only been bettered from the River Nene in the last ten years, but that aside it was some years before a river carp from anywhere in the country was caught near the weight of Beta's fish. Yet again, the Leney carp

# 6 SAVAY – THE ULTIMATE CHALLENGE

*Forty years of 'Leney' fish.*

## THE PONDS ARE DUG

Savay Lake at Harefield in Middlesex is an important part of the current carp fishing scene, and is perhaps the most enduring and readily fishable water out of those covered within this book. As I write it has produced more than forty carp of over 30lb in weight during this season alone! That puts it at the very pinnacle, for there is no other water in England I can think of which is currently capable of producing these sheer numbers of huge carp. At the top end it has produced three carp over 40lb in weight, and in common with most carp waters during the last few years the fish are seemingly getting bigger all the time...

Savay was originally stocked with literally thousands of carp during the 1950s, although not all of these were from the Donald Leney stable. The development of the fishery, its importance within carp fishing history and the anglers who fished there are as fascinating as they are famous.

It's not hard to understand how Savay originally came into existence. Its roots are the same as those of some twenty-five other pits, all dug from a rich seam of sand and gravel and which extended in a huge sweeping arch from Watford, and then travelled south through Rickmansworth, Gerrards Cross and Harefield, and finally ended due south of Heathrow Airport. The legacy left by these vast earth-moving projects have given angling, and particularly the carp fisher, a wealth of water and big carp to fish for ever since.

The original trial ponds dug at Savay Farm date from 1934, but these were small compared

to the ultimate size of the lake. In 1950, when the Ruislip Angling Society took control, the water consisted of two areas – the North and South waters. Digging then commenced west of this area where a large meadow was situated which

*Early aerial picture of Savay Lake. Moorfield Road is seen running at a forty-five-degree angle at the bottom of the picture. The large Cottage Bay is on the right complete with Lagoon area, and the North Bay is on the left. The partially joined Ruislip Island can be seen running down the centre.*

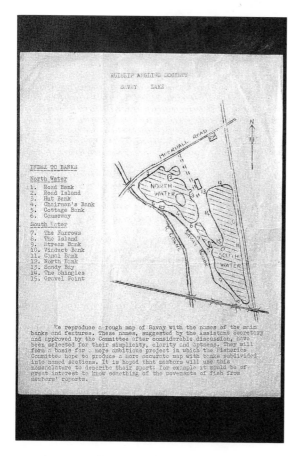

*Original map of Savay showing clearly the separate North and South waters.*

ined, this mammoth task meant that literally tons of gravel were physically moved by club members. The island is actually called the Ruislip Island and can only be fished by club members. The North Bay was one of the last to be finished and photographs of the day show gravel-washing equipment, a large hopper and conveyor belts all at work off Alcatraz (a peninsula of land that provides a boundary to the North Bay).

All gravel extractions were completed by 1973, but the Ruislip club had far from finished with their prize water. Landscaping was undertaken, with many trees being planted. Along the canal bank in accordance with the agreement (part of the indenture), the club was also to erect a fence of barbed wire, 4ft 6in high with four strands of wire along this boundary fence. The length was in the region of some 800yd, so willow stakes were driven into the bank. As these were live stakes they soon became established and eventually turned into trees, with some trunks growing 12in across! The stream bank was always a problem as it was a narrow piece of land washed from both sides, so to speak. However all the weakened areas were, over the years, modified and repaired until all was well.

The greatest effect the Ruislip Angling Society had on this fishery was through its far-reaching

*Looking from the North Bay down to the railway viaduct.*

divided the main River Colne and a small feeder stream called Savay Brook. This whole area of land belonged to a gentleman named Mr F. I. Cakebread, the owner of Savay Farm. Mr Cakebread sold this meadow, the extraction being carried out by Inns and Company. A series of small islands roughly following the old feeder stream were left, and the diggings to the north eventually joined up to the North Water itself. This made Savay complete, giving close on 70 acres of water.

In the early 1960s a major change was instigated by the Ruislip Angling Society. This was to make the series of little islands – which were originally joined by railway sleepers and duckboards – into a long, continuous island. As can be imag-

water management policy. This never happened on waters like Redmire, Billing or Frensham, but the policies carried out by the Ruislip club in the 1950s through to the 1970s gives us the unique water we have today.

The Club Secretary in the period of 1965 to 1975 was Mike Wilson (Savay's greatest historian), and he and the Water Management Committee practised a very rigid policy of unwanted fish removal. They followed the advice of Mr F. Page, a noted ichthyologist, and later the advice of biologist Dr Charles Franklin. In a letter dated 22 March 1950, Mr Page states: 'Deep waters produce bigger and better fish providing there are shallow parts for weed to grow. The Gravel pits around Rickmansworth ought to produce the best fishing in the country.' Interesting that, in the light of what actually happened!

Early nettings however, showed poor growth rates due to a lack of food and food production areas. To improve the lake, fertilizer in the shape of pig manure was administered every close season. The water was rigorously netted to remove all small roach and bream so that more food was hopefully left for the carp. This was hard work, but with plenty of hands on deck the job was usually successfully completed. A giant net, well over 100yd in length and 10ft deep with a cod end in its centre was used for the purpose.

The Club Chairman, Gerry Love, usually laid the net by rowing out in a great wide circle. Only the float lines were pulled, the lead lines being allowed to follow the bed of the lake. Sometimes the results were poor – a few pike and roach – but often they hit the jackpot with thousands upon thousands of small roach and perch. The bulk of these was tipped straight into the River Colne.

What filled the void created by the regular removal of the unwanted species? You guessed it – carp!

## TWO HUNDRED AND EIGHT CARP

We have to turn back the clock to 1950 to find out how the Leney carp came to be stocked into Savay. Again, the foresight of the club in

stocking with carp when few others did was indeed a good move. The original invoice of November 1950 shows that 208 king carp of 3–4in (one-year old) were bought, for which the club paid £35-5-0d (£35.25). By November 1954, odd carp were caught up to 4lb in weight showing that some growth had taken place. The pit was still being worked at this stage and the water was clouded for much of the time, hence there was little in the way of natural weed growth or food. These carp would be in their fourth year and showed rather poor growth rates, especially for king carp. The following December (1951), a further 300 king carp were shipped to Savay. These too were one-year-old fish and came from the same sort of 'year class' that went into Frensham and the Electricity Cut.

All was left quiet with these fish, for no one fished for them specifically and anyway Savay received little in the way of real angling pressure during the 1950s. This lack of angling pressure combined with an escalating food supply meant that the fish were able to grow much better during the latter half of the 1950s. By 1963 the best carp recorded weighed 23lb 8oz, and this might actually have been the first recorded twenty-pounder from the lake. It was also in this period that more carp from the Surrey Trout Farm were purchased. The first in 1965 consisted of 200 4–6in kings, then a further 200 of similar size were bought in 1968. These, coupled with the earlier stockings of 1950 and 1951, gave a grand

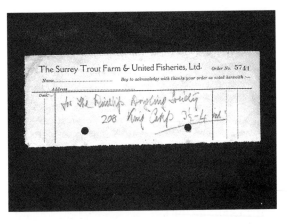

*Surrey Trout Farm invoice for Savay showing 208 kings.*

total of some 900 king carp! Every single one with the potential to be an English record breaker...

As the emerging years of carp fishing unfolded, many anglers started to fish for carp at Savay in the early 1960s. Although most just fell into carp fishing, others seemed to be destined for it. One such angler was Mike Wilson, whose catches throughout the 1970s at Savay were spectacular to say the least, but which were largely unrecorded at the time because of the publicity ban in force by the Ruislip club. The recognition for these catches came much later, and I seem to remember that few people believed Mike even then – in fact, it was only when Mike's superb photographic work came to the fore that the catches proved to be every bit as good as the stories. Mike's early tussles with Savay carp are as exciting as they are innocent. Here are his thoughts on his introduction to a water that was to dominate his life for more than fifteen years.

'The first time I ever fished Savay was in the early 1960s. I'd just started work and was invited to join the Ruislip Angling Society by friends Rex and John. Rex and I fished for all species but our imagination was fired by carp and the published results of the Carp Catchers' Club.

'Arriving in my A40 Somerset and parking in a car-park which looked rather like craters on the moon, the gravel diggings being in full progress, I decided to fish just past the Cottage point, casting out to the swallows. Bits of barbed wire could be seen sticking out of the water at this point. They were the visible remains of the old stream bank fence, odd areas being criss-crossed with them and occasionally catching in the club's net during working parties. This day there were, I think, two or three carp breaking the surface. They weren't big by today's standard, but to my companion Rex and I they were enormous. In retrospect, they were probably in the region of 15lb. The bow wave they made was something I had, at the time, never seen before. In my innocence, they looked easy to catch if I could get a crust to them.

'I used 12lb BS line, no lead and a piece of "dunked" crust the size of a matchbox. Could I

reach them? Could I heck! It was really frustrating. However, as the light went down I fished the crust in the margins in true "Walker" style and promptly caught my first Savay tench!

'An hour or so later I was just able to see some ripples coming out from the bank. Suspecting carp (I hoped), I recast a fresh crust into the area and sat well back to await events. They weren't long in coming! Movements in the reeds, followed by what appeared to be a jerky-type run, had me over the rod. I struck and felt nothing except something brush past my face. It was my line. Not quite realizing what had happened, I started to reel in the slack until I felt movement. It was a damn great angry rat. Uncertain what to do, I kept the line tight and almost immediately it broke, or was bitten through, the rat taking refuge in Mr Watson's cottage back garden just behind me. I suppose it was a couple of firsts – my first bite-off and my first rat!

'The early years at Savay were a failure for me as regards carp. I lacked, as indeed did so many others, the tackle to cope with such a large water. Baits were also an enigma. I was limited to the main four – bread in its various forms, potatoes, worms and pastes of dubious contents. The lack of knowledge meant that I only carp fished when I saw the fish, which was rare.

'It wasn't long before I asked to join the Water Management Committee and, during my period on it, we introduced a lot of carp. Slowly the carp stocks were improving and after regularly seeing them, I started carp fishing again. Bread I found useless and paste baits never failed to attract the attentions of the bream. I had runs on potatoes, it's true, but can't with all honesty suggest they were ever from carp (but they did catch many tench). Around the late 1960s, when the Long Island was joined to what is now known as Alcatraz, there was a small ridge off the causeway with true bulrushes on it; the depth my side was about 2ft 6in, whilst the water dropped off to 9ft past the bulrushes. I fished it many times by 'laying on' with a green-painted swan quill and lobworms as bait. I caught a lot of tench, but one day a 'tench' went off with so much power that I began to wonder afterwards what I'd lost!

*A selection of the Leney record books. The whole collection was passed on to Chris Yates after Donald Leney's death in 1987. They hold many secrets…*

All three of these personally hand-built Richard Walker split cane Mk IV carp rods saw duty at Redmire Pool. Pictured left is the rod that beat the record 44lb common in September 1952.

'They threw away the mould after this one.' An immaculate unmarked linear (line mirror), landed by the author in the summer of 1985.

*Common carp – although scant within the stocking of Leney carp in the UK – are nevertheless just as desirable. Andy Little with a lovely twenty-pounder dating back to 1984.*

*Andy Thomas holds a beautifully scaled Frensham carp caught by his friend Kevin Grozier on a piece of crust from the loaf behind!*

*Brett White shows off a fine example of a classical Galician. This heavily plated mirror tipped the scales at 25lb.*

*A rare Dick Walker colour photograph of Redmire Pool in the mid-1950s.*

*Redmire as it looks these days, still a magical water.*

*Don Smith displays a heavily scaled Frensham mirror that came during wet weather. Don only ever fished there once, but he caught this 24lb beauty and went away happy saying, 'It's unlikely I'll ever catch a more beautiful carp.'*

*Andy Little with one of Redmire's old, gorgeous-looking linear mirrors. It is a credit to all the anglers who have landed this specimen and who treat fish care with prime importance.*

*The Redmire scales. These were purchased by the original Redmire syndicate which Jack Hilton headed in 1968. The box was made by noted big carp man Roger Smith. Among the many big carp that have been hoisted aloft on to these scales was Chris Yates' current record 51lb 8oz mirror.*

*A terrific picture of Mike Wilson with a superlative Savay mirror, taken amid the baiting pyramid campaign.*

*Savay Lake photographed by Mike Wilson in the late 1970s.*

*A lightly scaled mirror of over 30lb…with dimensions of 33in to the fork of the tail and a girth of 26in.*

*Rod Hutchinson with a gold and red coloured winter mirror from Savay.*

*Amongst the development of tackle specifically designed for large carp was the design of a light, collapsible landing net.*
*This model (which dates from the early 1950s) was hand-built in bamboo cane by noted carp angler Derrick Davenport.*
*It is a replica of Dick Walker's own net which Derrick had borrowed one close season.*

*This style of scaling –
along the lateral line as
well as scales just above
and below – was often in
evidence in the mirrors.
This is yet another fine
carp from Frensham.*

*This carp, landed by
Andy Little in October
1984, had a length of
35in to the fork of the
tail!*

*A fully scaled mirror for Tim Paisley from Horseshoe Lake in 1991.*

*Modern young Leney carp from the Carp Society's Horseshoe Lake:* above, *an immaculate fifteen-pounder;* below, *a 17lb linear mirror.*

*Clarissa, Dick Walker's record 44-pounder, immortalized in a wood carving by Brian Mills. This life-size trophy was struck by the Carp Society in 1988 as a permanent memorial to Richard Walker. The author was the first recipient.*

*Actual scales from Clarissa. These were given to the author by Paul Bray who worked at the shop where the cased carp was displayed. Clarissa died at the London Zoo Aquarium in May 1971 having lived there since September 1952.*

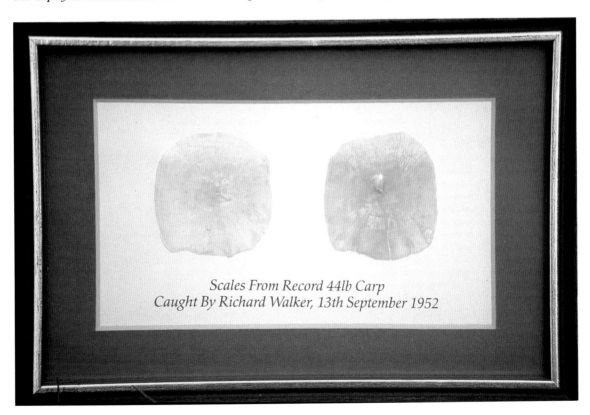

Scales From Record 44lb Carp
Caught By Richard Walker, 13th September 1952

*Chris Yates with the record carp – another perfect linear.*

*Future big carp? Tiny Galician offspring of Redmire carp that are becoming available through the Castle Carp Company.*

'During the autumn I was again on the Long Island, just past the walkway on the right-hand side. I was float fishing with lobworms in 8ft of water. The fishing was slow and I thought of moving down a swim or two. I went to inspect the swims, not bothering to reel in. What a mistake! When I returned a couple of minutes later, I was dismayed to see all the line run out on one of the rods. On reeling in, there was nothing there, but it prompted me into action. I started carp fishing in earnest, using worms and mussels as bait.

'Over the next few years I fished dozens of swims, looking for the ideal one. What I did learn was that if I fished just any old swim I caught tench and bream, plus the odd pike and perch. When I fished shallow water up to, say, 3ft I had far less trouble with other species except, of course, tench. The important thing was that I not only saw odd carp on the shallows, but I also had the odd run.

'The most successful early swim was the island by the cottage entrance. I used to sit on a sack inside a heavy-duty carrier bag on the ground. The first island didn't have the space for a chair, plus the height of me would have scared the fish, I'm sure. I hid behind a few sparse reeds and dock I had planted for cover. Casting had to be sideways to get any distance, and I had to be very careful as the bottom dropped away sharply and I can swim like a brick! The baits were cast into the gaps of the tiny island and Road Bank Island on hard gravel. Apart from lobworms and mussels, no other bait was used in case it attracted other fish. Rods were set very low down with the tips just out of the water. Indicators were rings of silver paper and, because of the problem of plant growth, I used a 2ft square canvas groundsheet to rest the indicators on.

'I fished the water regularly after work until dark to no avail, until one evening my right-hand indicator shot into the butt ring and I struck. Straight through the gap the fish went, and my line was well and truly hung up in the branches on the tiny island. This problem happened time and again...I became desperate. I thought I had to get very heavy-handed with the fish, and one lunchtime popped into a small tackle shop which

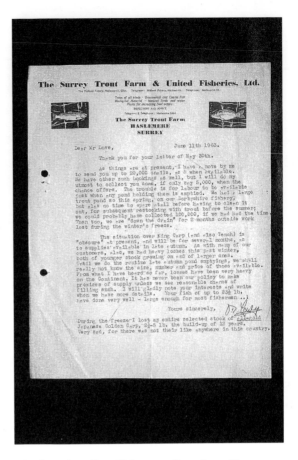

*This letter from Donald Leney to Gerry Love (then Chairman of Ruislip Angling Club) reveals several interesting points. First, it shows how the severity of the 1962/3 winter had affected stocks both here and abroad, and second, it mentions that a 23lb 8oz carp had been caught. This fish was the best Savay had produced at the time.*

existed where Keith Sellick's Middlesex Angling Centre now is. The chap sold me what he called a bass rod. It was a 10ft compound rod with a test curve of, I'd guess, around 2lb. I used it in conjunction with my trusty Cardinal 66s and 12lb BS line. It worked on my very next trip and I caught a fish of 18lb 8oz – at the time, my best. I was delighted; four lobs on a size 2 Goldstrike caused its downfall. The hooks were overthick, but far more reliable than the speedbarbs I had previously used.

*Cliff Glenton, whose carp-catching exploits go back into the 1950s, was an early angler who realized Savay's carp potential.*

'The next evening, before starting to fish, I walked down to the Cottage Point and found Cliff Glenton and Alex Rennie fishing out towards the shallows. Now, Cliff and Alex were old members and had a reasonable amount of success at Savay and elsewhere. They kept their fishing very much to themselves, but opened up a bit when I told them of my fish of the previous

*This was Mike Wilson's first Savay carp. It came from the small island in the end corner of the cottage bay – in truth he should not have been there!*

evening. Whilst I understand they had tried various baits, it was significant to note that on the ground was a large silver tin with blue writing (which I recognized as a ration-time dried milk tin). Inside was a pile of lobworms. At least I was on the right track...

'Then it happened. It was Saturday in early August and I'd just bought a Morris Oxford in anticipation of a rush to the hospital because my wife was expecting. It was a fabulously warm evening with a slight mist. I had the lake to myself and went on to the usual Cottage Island. I only had lobworms for bait, but stopped and picked a dozen or so swan mussels which were always to be found in the sandy mud round the island. Worms were fished to the left hand of the tiny island and swan mussels to the right. I then made

myself comfortable for the night and awaited events as I'd done many times before.

The mist cleared in the morning and the sun came up, straight in my face. It was hot, even at 5 a.m., and I had stripped to my T-shirt. There was no movement at all, except from the bees and flies. About 6.30 a.m. I saw a 'postage stamp', a term I used for the showing tip of a carp's dorsal fin, moving from the right towards me. The fish was not in a hurry and took perhaps half an hour before she was in my swim. All of a sudden, in only 2ft of water, its tail came partially out as it up-ended and fed. I realized it was only a few feet from my swan mussel bait and, within seconds, checked that my line was clear of any obstruction and everything was ready – just in case. Silently, the indicator moved slowly to the butt ring and fell back to the groundsheet as line spilled off the spool. It rose again and, on checking everything again, I clamped my left hand over the open spool and struck.

'On hooking, the fish went on a blistering run out into the Cottage Bay. I hated trusting slipping clutches in those days, and after closing the bail arm let the reel backwind. It did, catching my thumb in the process. Keeping the rod as high as possible to avoid the line touching those damned Zebra mussels, I applied as much pressure as I dared. The fish stopped taking line and kited to my right to the Cottage Point.

'I'd like to continue saying it was a spectacular fight, but I would be lying. Grudgingly the fish came towards me as I started pumping her and praying the hook wouldn't tear out, break, line part and all those other horrible thoughts that go through one's mind when you know you are playing your best ever fish.

'Eventually, the fish was under the rod point and after a few anxious moments in the reeds which fringed the island, I netted and dragged it to the bank. For me, in those early years, it looked huge and bigger than anything I'd seen before at Savay or, indeed, anywhere else. My thumb was still throbbing from being clouted by the reel handle and my heart must have thought I had run a marathon. I couldn't stop shaking as I fumbled for a cigarette and my Salter 40lb scales.

'All sorts of things went through my mind as the scales were lifted in the landing-net mesh. Weighing the fish wasn't easy, as I was still in the water due to space restriction and had to lift the scales to head height with my aching arms resisting all the way. The scales read 27lb and, allowing for the net mesh, I was happy to call her 26lb.

'I stood looking at the gasping fish for a few moments with genuine tearful eyes. If only my old school friend, Rex, could have seen this. He'd emigrated to Australia a couple of years previous and, although we had planned to meet up again in future years, it was not to be as he was killed in a car accident.

'My camera was one of those "new" instamatic jobs and I rattled off a few shots, each one embarrassingly poor. With the fish on the ground it looked nothing and, not long after, I resolved to get a decent camera and learn a bit more about photography. After reluctantly returning the fish (I wanted to look at it all day), I packed up and drove home, reliving the capture in my mind over and over again. The club rules were very strict, and being an official I for one couldn't break them without the obvious consequence of suspension. I wanted to tell the world what I'd caught but couldn't and the angling press rarely had such a fish recorded. The pictures turned out dreadful, which perhaps was meant to be as they could never have been published.'

## GROWN-UP CARP

In Mike Wilson's tale he makes mention of Cliff Glenton and Alex Rennie, both of whom were experienced anglers and carp fishers in the true sense of the word. Cliff, besides being the one-time proprietor of the famous West London tackle shop of B. James & Son, had been a keen and successful carp fisherman since the 1950s. Cliff had accounted for his first 20lb carp way back in 1959 from another Middlesex water. Alex was also a carp fisherman who had fished the famous Wadhurst Lake in Sussex. Together, these two were some of the first anglers to harness the potential of the big carp at Savay. They had accounted for a number of good double-figure fish in the early 1970s, but they had seen far larger than they'd caught. It must be remembered that to catch a carp approaching 20lb in those days was quite something, and often drew a big picture and report in the angling press.

By the mid 1970s many of the Savay carp from the original Leney stocking of 1951 and 1952 were mature fish. A greater percentage were all well over 20lb in weight, with the best likely to have topped 30lb. However, the crazy thing was that few realized this – it seems that the phenomenal rise in popularity that carp fishing saw in this period had largely passed Savay by. This was almost certainly due to the strict 'No Publicity' rule that was in force. Saying that, it did not stop the process of 'by word of mouth' that inevitably took place locally, but carp were still considered in many people's eyes as fairly uncatchable. Whatever the reason, the carp at Savay had somewhat of a quiet life, although the odd fish was hooked and landed in the regular matches that took place at the time.

It was against this backdrop that Mike Wilson, who had come of age in carp fishing, started a campaign against the elusive and large fish present. Using extensive close season observations he tried to pin-point areas where the carp would be. The first area, as Mike explained in his account, was the Cottage Island, then he tried further along the cottage road where Cliff Glenton often fished (this is out of bounds these days). But Mike was to find other likely spots well away from the Cottage Bay part of the lake. The North Bay revealed a bottom full of contours that was worth more than a cursory look. The long east bank, named the Canal Bank, showed a myriad of features in the shape of long, continuous gravel bars, humps, plateaux and gullies that appeared throughout this vast area of water. However, it was in an area some 60–70yd down the Canal Bank, close to a small island and almost opposite the end of Alcatraz, that Mike found a superb spot close in.

He figured that this part of the lake fell into line with his thoughts on how carp travel on the wind. In previous winters on a lake close by (West Hyde) he only caught on a south-westerly wind, or should I say he only had bites in those conditions. He looked for the same set of circumstances on Savay and found that the prevailing south-westerly hit the Canal Bank and drove up into the North Bay. It was then a case of looking for a feature – he didn't have to look very far, for there just in the right position was an island. This island was not very big, maybe 12–15ft across and sported a couple of little willows with trailing roots going into the water. It was situated some 25ft or so from the bank and the water between was unusually deep – maybe 12–14ft. It was full of all kinds of debris: small branches, dead brambles and accumulated rubbish, in fact it was a right tangled mess. Mike had actually fished in amongst this area, for on one trip he'd seen a

*Rods at the ready – possibly Clive Diedrich's?*

huge swirl which might have been a pike, but which could have been a carp…

He plumbed the immediate area and found that the margins of the island slowly fell away on all sides. However, from the back of the island this slope was very gradual all the way out to the point of Alcatraz. But it was to the left of the island, parallel with the Canal Bank, that Mike found the most interesting features. Here the water fell away slowly from the island then suddenly descended much quicker, down to 12ft for a number of yards, then came up again to end in a smallish plateau close to the surface of the water. Here was a hump in the lake's bottom with deeper water all round – Mike had found a hot spot.

He tried his already successful baits – worms and swan mussels – in this area, but the last thing he caught was carp. Indeed, tench made a perfect nuisance of themselves taking the bait time after time. It was the change to a special paste bait that resulted in the first carp from 'Wilson's Island'. This paste was being used by his friends at West Hyde and included amongst the ingredients was Phillip's Yeast Mix (PYM). At this time (the mid-1970s) there were huge developments underway in terms of baits and flavours, with Fred Wilton and his friends showing the way with catches the carp world thought at the time were impossible. These were called high-protein baits. Many people started to experiment along these lines, and in Mike Wilson's case this was to lead to him later (in association with Clive Diedrich) forming the bait company called E. S. Reding.

## PARTICLES!

The biggest turning point with bait at Savay was not the special PYM paste, however, but another much published method that caught Mike's eye at the time – particles.

Articles appeared in monthly fishing magazines of the day from the likes of Rod Hutchinson (who wrote several) and Kent angler, Paul Snepp, on the use of small, identical sized baits like black-eyed beans, chick peas, soya beans and, of course sweetcorn. It was sweetcorn that Mike wanted to try, but just to make it different to that used by other people, he flavoured it.

The original idea of this flavouring came from the stories of Bob Reynolds' Billing captures, where he had stated that he had used banana flavour. Not content with going to the local delicatessen for a household flavour in a small jar, Mike contacted Enco – a manufacturer of a good banana flavour – and after a while couldn't get enough of the stuff! Mike had a friend who worked for the freezer superstore Bejam and he bought huge amounts of sweetcorn. To start with he only applied a small amount of banana flavouring to the corn. Mike remembers that this flavour, although smelling realistic, was bitter to taste. He was playing around with all kinds of dosages, eventually building up to a point when the corn really did smell of bananas. However, in these kinds of concentrations he found that the stronger the flavour, the less he caught. The secret, therefore, was to put just enough in so that the merest hint of banana flavour could be smelt. Another important extra ingredient was added sugar. Mike worked out that this needed to be invert sugar, and to give that acid effect he also included a squeeze of lemon to the mix of sweetcorn, banana flavour and sugar.

Initially, he would go fishing on a Friday night when more often than not he would have the place to himself – it was rare ever to have anyone else fishing. He would always put out a reasonable amount of bait because one of the early problems was takes from bream. As he was always worried that a few bream would come in the swim and take half the bait, he just kept piling the sweetcorn out.

Terminal tackle was another area about which Mike had positive views. At the time, most people free-lined with no weight whatsoever on the line. Mike, by contrast, used a link ledger. This two swan shot link was only a couple of inches long and was stopped some 4in from the hook itself, this being a size 4 or 6 holding two or three grains of corn.

Then the catches started. Big fish were amongst these, with a number of fish over 25lb and the average size was extremely high, with few being caught below 20lb in weight. Also, there was little in the way of repeat captures as Savay had so many carp swimming around. Then the money started to run out – Mike was married with two small babies and a mortgages, and the cost of buying sweetcorn (in bulk freezer bags) was getting too much to bear – money was tight. Alternatives were soon to come his way, but in the meantime, the catches in 1977 alone were simply staggering: one catch of four twenty-pounders in a night and then incredibly a five-fish catch again with four over 20lb in weight. All these came from Wilson's Island which, as we have found, was not in fact the Island swim, but lay 10yd to the left on or around the plateau. In those days it really was a delightful spot, with high reeds obscuring the angler from the water and, more importantly, the fish. The reeds were parted just enough to leave a gap for the rod tips to poke through. Because of the closeness of the baited area – approximately 10yd or in winter even closer – Mike was also extremely quiet. In fact I've known Mike personally for many years now and he won't mind me saying this: he is naturally a quiet person and moves around without hardly a sound.

It was during this period that the outside world started to get to hear about these extraordinary carp captures, although Mike had tried to keep all this pretty hush-hush. It happened that two anglers from Yorkshire were down fishing as a guest of Tim Goode at West Hyde. As can be imagined, at that time, Yorkshire's waters were far from being overrun with 20lb carp! Kevin Roberts and John Morrel were the anglers concerned, and they met Mike at West Hyde. He happened to mention that he'd caught some twenty-pounders, and said that in fact he was just off to get some photographs of a catch of *four in a night*. The Yorkshire anglers blinked, looked at one another disbelievingly, then asked whether they could see the historic photographs. They followed Mike home and pored over the pictures.

In Mike's eyes many of the photographs were poor – it must be remembered that he had sorted out the photographic side of his fishing and was by then using a high quality 2¼in Yashica camera. Even so, he was often very critical of his own photographic work; pictures that look wonderful to you and me were rejected on the grounds of slightly poor exposure or that the depth of field was minutely out. However, that said, the photographs rejected by Mike were, after discussion, given to Kevin Roberts and John Morrel with the strict instructions that the venue should not be revealed. If they kept their word they could fish with Mike at the lake. They wrote on the back of these prints 'Yavas' the code name for Savay – which, you might have worked out, is the word Savay written backwards!

These two Yorkshire anglers were due back at West Hyde that evening and Mike asked them that if he had the good fortune to catch a 20lb carp that night at Savay, would they like to see it? You can guess the reply. That night Mike's luck was in again, and come dawn he had a 20lb 8oz leather carp in the sack. He went over to West Hyde and found the two anglers...fast asleep. They came with Mike and photographed the fish.

Kevin Roberts was a leading light in the north at the time, a good angler who could catch carp all the year round, beside being a staunch British Carp Study Group member and a friend of Kevin Clifford. Kevin saw these photos as did Rod Hutchinson. Rod remembers viewing these pictures at the time: 'We were trying to work out where Yavas was – we knew it must be some water!'

Another local angler also started fishing Savay around this time, and his name was Clive Diedrich. Clive's carp fishing had started some years earlier, and the first set of proper carp rods he acquired were bought off me. That set Clive on the road to big fish from which he never looked back. Whether it was the rods that did the trick I'll never know...maybe I should have kept them! Anyway, he turned up one night at Savay and started fishing near the lagoon on the road bank. Mike Wilson was there and was somewhat surprised to find another angler fishing. Mike had caught a carp that evening which Clive had witnessed, and in fact Mike caught another while Clive was talking to him.

During the next few weeks Mike was catching carp hand over fist, and most of them weighed over 20lb. To Clive (and to everyone else) these carp hauls were extraordinary; needless to say it did not take too long for Clive to start catching and a friendship started between these two. Clive went on to catch many of the Savay carp (including some very big ones) and continued to fish for Savay carp for longer than Mike Wilson eventually did.

Gary Whitehorn and Terry Clarke were other successful Ruislip members on the water. I remember talking to these gentlemen when we met up at British Carp Study Group meetings, but I was largely unaware that their wonderful pictures and the stories they told me of big carp were in fact Savay fish. They, too, held everything close to their chests. However, you could hardly blame them or any of the fishermen I've already mentioned for this, for Savay was special – very special indeed.

The first 30lb carp was captured from Savay in 1978, but it wasn't taken by Mike Wilson as most people thought was the case. When I met Mike recently, he told me he knew the person who had landed this large carp, but couldn't remember his name. This fisherman evidently only fished for one season, never to return!

## THE BAITING PYRAMID

The close season of 1979 saw Mike and Clive looking for different particles to use as bait, because sweetcorn, in the supply that they needed, worked out far too expensive. Maize was the one they settled for. It was the start of a bonanza of catches the likes of which the carp world had rarely seen before. Again, in the Canal Bank hot spot Mike started baiting extremely heavily. It was apparent to Mike through his previous two years' fishing that the more bait he put in, the more he caught and with seemingly bigger fish all the time.

He put his views on this down in a thought-provoking article that appeared in the first edition of *Carp Fisher*, the Carp Society's official (milestone) publication. It was called *The Baiting Pyramid* (1981), and it was received with a great deal of fuss. Mike has kindly allowed me to reprint it here.

'One of the big waters I fish regularly contains a head of carp from low doubles to thirty pound fish. There is nothing unusual about this as many large waters up and down the country are in the same category – where the controlling club had a regular stocking policy. Our problem was how to consistently pick out the better quality fish. Many rod hours can be spent on the fishery, and up to a point there is an element of luck as to the weight of the fish caught.

'Obviously, the experienced carp angler will get a greater number of takes over a season, and catch that many more fish. At the end of the day, by sheer numbers of fish on the bank, a proportion will be the better than average fish. As experience grows, so generally does the overall result. For anglers seeking the better fish any way of reducing the luck element is of prime importance.

'This article is based on my belief that anglers can be selective, and catch big fish by design from these large waters. My theory behind this belief is based on a characteristic found in many gregarious animals. This is the dominant position taken up by the sheer power and size over another species. It isn't quite, however, the bully syndrome found in man. That is due to lack of discipline and greed not normally found in the animal world. No, this is similar to the situation commonly found, for example, at a water-hole in Africa. During the day various herds of animals, driven by thirst, arrive at the water-hole. Each group, depending on how high it is in the "Pecking Order", either waits for others to finish or moves in and takes over the prime positions. This happens irrespective of the fact that they may be totally outnumbered. Finally a small herd of elephants may appear and although not predatory to (say) a herd of impala, their sheer size will oust the greater numbers of impala.

'Similar examples can be seen daily in the animal world. Watch birds feeding in your garden and note how some will dominate others. If we logically follow this through we can see how a large carp, or a group of large carp will dominate smaller fish in certain feeding situations.

*Mike Wilson with the results of the 'baiting pyramid'.*

*This small swim, just to the left of the little island on the canal bank, was the place where Mike Wilson made many of his famous catches in the late 1970s. Although enlarged somewhat these days it still carries the name of Wilson's.*

'I have watched, on a few occasions, a large shoal of fish up to low twenties. Each time when a smaller shoal of larger twenties decided to "move in" the large shoal moved away. These in turn moved out when an even smaller group of bigger fish decided that they wanted to feed. This cannot be just coincidence. Obviously I can only assume that this pattern is followed as a normal feeding routine. Subsequent results however, convinced me that this was so. I see no reason why this pattern shouldn't be followed in waters elsewhere, where fish range from low doubles upwards. On the waters I've fished it is also significant to note that the carp appear to shoal up "tighter" in autumn when the temperature drops. Catches of two, or three, or even more twenty-pound fish in a few hours have been comparatively common.

'Being convinced of the logic behind these facts and assumptions, the next problem was how to utilize this knowledge. I formulated a baiting programme which I termed as the Baiting Pyramid.

'I based the programme on the assumption that the longer I baited a swim the more fish would find it, in turn pushing the less dominant species out. Too much angling pressure in the early stages of baiting would spook them away and the bigger fish would move away. It was also important to get the maximum number of fish feeding, as the more fish that confidently fed on the bait, the less chance there was of spooking all the fish after hooking one.

'Having formulated the tactics I prepared for the experiment. I was fishing a big lake and, as can be expected, the fish would move around on the wind if the temperature was right. I had no intention of chasing the fish. Indeed, if the theory was right I had to get them to come to me.

'Choosing a swim on the east bank which was full of variable depth features (*Wilson's Island*), I started the baiting. It was the first week of August, not a particularly productive time in my experience. I baited daily with upwards of twenty pounds of maize. The maize was first soaked for twenty-four hours, then pressure cooked at fifteen pounds per square inch for half an hour. The process was then repeated. Any further additions or attractors were "boiled in" for twenty minutes just prior to baiting up or fishing.

'The twenty minutes is purely arbitrary, and is dependent on how soft you require the final bait. Maize was chosen for a number of reasons. Bearing in mind the amount I intended to use over the three months or so, cost was paramount. Secondly I doubted whether there were many others who would be prepared to go to the trouble of preparing it. It really can be an absolute pain doing this every day.

*Mike Wilson supports Sally the Carp, a carp he caught a number of times.*

'I like a very soft bait to begin with as this attracts the roach and bream. I've found that constant activity of feeding bream acts as an attractor in itself. I've lost count of the number of times I've finally caught a carp after ploughing through the bream all night. Unlike many I do not object to catching the odd bream if this eventually brings about the desired result.

'As it happened my wife got bait production off to a fine art, cooking large quantities during the day. Incidentally I cannot subscribe to the view that fermenting maize is better for carp. I've only had limited success with it. This also applies to all the legumes I've used.

'Six weeks after the start of the programme a couple of evenings were spent in the swim to see how the bait was working. The evenings were cold with a North-westerly wind. I didn't expect much but was well pleased with three fish to eighteen pounds. The baiting programme was beginning to work. If the theory was right I could expect better fish as they pushed the others out. Each night I watched the water for a while after baiting up. There certainly appeared to be plenty of activity judging by the heavy rocking water coming back to me.

'Constant baiting and not overfishing the swim for fear of spooking them, meant I "held" the fish for a further six weeks. It would have been so easy to have fished the swim each night, as the water had little carp angling pressure, but I doubted the wisdom of such actions. It was interesting to note that on the nights I fished I had more than one chance, and multiple catches were almost the norm. As can be expected the bites were not much more than one or two inch pulls, denoting very confident fish. This suited my style of fishing as I prefer to strike at any movement at all.

'Because of this I failed to hit a few early bites due to the lack of sensitivity of my Optonics. This was soon overcome by making breaker wheels out of milk bottle tops with eight blades instead of the customary four. Another tactic I have used with these delicate bites is to put the Optonic beyond the rod tip. But this requires a lot of messing about setting up, not to mention a reasonable amount of bank space, which I rarely have.

'Strangely, I cannot ever remember having a bite-off. This may have been due to my tactics as I know of others who have been bitten off. A change

*Clive Diedrich, with a good fish from the 'Dutch' stocking.*

in terminal rig would, no doubt, have encouraged runs, but at the time there was little need.

'During the period of this experiment I amassed a total of twenty-three fish; ten doubles, seven low/mid twenties, culminating in six carp over twenty-nine pounds. The last, a low thirty, being taken a day before frosts put paid to my carp fishing for the autumn.

'It may all have been luck of course, and I might be totally wrong on the theory. However I have tried it on a different water and am now convinced in my own mind that this is one way of sorting out the larger fish from big waters.'

This proved to be Mike Wilson's finest hour, but also marked the beginning of the end of his incredible run of big fish and of his exclusive fishing of a water on which he had literally grown up. The reason? The mighty 'Redlands'. These were the Ruislip club's and, in turn, the Savay's landlords who were to promote a more open policy towards whose who could fish their waters.

## REDLAND'S RULE OK

Before I look at this important development at Savay, another episode comes to mind that revealed the potential of Savay to a famous Lincolnshire carp angler.

In 1979 Rod Hutchinson was, for a period, living and fishing at Kodak Lake (now Harefield) in Middlesex. He and his older brother were working in London during the day, they came to Kodak and fished all night in their bivvies (home), went to work the next day...and so on. Rod's brother was a fitness fanatic and on their return in the evening he would often go for a run along the tow-path of the local canal. One evening upon his return he couldn't find Rod anywhere near his bivvy. Then Rod whistled – he was aloft in a nearby tree, gesturing to his brother to come up the tree. His brother was soon by his side. 'Look at these big carp here,' said Rod, pointing down into the water. 'If you think they're big,' said his brother, 'come and see what I've just found.'

Rod followed his brother down the tow-path of the canal, and there through the gaps in the trees was a lake. Quietly nipping through the frail fence they were soon climbing a tree over the spot where his brother had seen the fish earlier. Sure enough there they were, half a dozen big carp cruising around. As the pair looked from their tree-top position at this large, overgrown lake, Rod commented that no one was about and neither were there signs of the place having been fished. Perhaps, thought Rod, a little bit of 'guesting' was in order – under the cover of darkness of course. Unwittingly, Rod and his brother had found 'Yavas', or should I say Savay!

A couple of nights later Rod moved in once it was dark. The area he chose was but a few feet from Wilson's Island. Out went his trusty bait – black-eyed beans – and, come the morning, Rod had three carp under his belt. The best was a 23lb mirror, with the others weighing in at 18lb and 19lb. With this success, he planned a return the following night...

This time he sat for a long while without so much as a bleep from his indicators. It was a still night, one where the slightest sound could be heard. Suddenly Rod did hear a sound, although

*Malcolm Winkworth with his first twenty-pounder from Savay. This lovely fish was caught in November 1979.*

some way off, of someone coming along the bank. (I personally think this might have been Mike Wilson coming to bait up!) Anyway, in a flash Rod was packed up and through the fence in double-quick time. Back at Kodak Lake Rod thought he'd give 'guesting' the water a rest for a day or two, but events were to catch up with him before then. The following evening there appeared on the banks of Kodak a slim, medium-height man dressed in dark green. He seemed to be looking for someone. With few anglers on the lake it didn't take long to find Rod Hutchinson's bivvy. Looking at the rod set-up he knew he'd found the angler he was looking for.

Looking at Rod he said, 'I know you've been fishing our water and you're not a member.'

'How do you know that?' asked Rod.

'It's your set-up, those indicator needles,' said the stranger.

'That's impossible,' said Rod.

'No, I'm right,' said the club official.

It appeared that in his haste Rod had left his vertical needle indicators behind in the ground at Savay. No one at that time and in that part of the world used vertical needles (especially not ones that took specially fashioned wine-top indicators) except him!

It was a fair cop, and Rod admitted (eventually) to the crime. Guess who had tugged him – it was Mike Wilson! Afterwards Rod realized that the water he'd guested on was Savay (Yavas). But how could he have known? Quite simply, he recognized Mike Wilson from the picture he had seen from the year before, the one Kevin Roberts had shown him!

In early 1980 the first whispers that Savay Lake was being offered as a one-off syndicate for one year were circulating. Few people realized the significance of this, and the innermost circle of carp anglers were the only ones to appreciate this once-in-a-lifetime offer. I remember this being discussed (in hushed tones at Ritchie McDonald's house) after a British Carp Study Group's meeting at Staines near London. It was talked of by Redlands as an all-out effort to see what the water held. The rest is as they say, history and one that has been well documented. However, I would like to look at some of the highlights of that history-making 1980 season.

*John Baker and a 30lb mirror caught during the first year of the Savay syndicate in 1980.*

*Andy Little on opening day 1980 with a big framed thirty-pounder. He went on to take forty-three carp over 20lb during that season!*

*Rod Hutchinson with a 1980 thirty-pounder. Rod went on to catch many others.*

The anglers who formed this syndicate were split into two rotas – one week on, one week off and were dedicated carp anglers. They included the likes of Andy Little, Clive Diedrich, Lenny Middleton, Geoff Kemp, John Baker, Kevin Maddocks and a host of others, including Albert Romp, Roger Smith, Mike Wilson and Rod Hutchinson – he'd somehow got back in favour!

Can you begin to imagine how Mike Wilson viewed all this? These were heavy carp anglers and all were keen to try their luck. Opening night saw Andy Little settle in next to Mike. Andy was armed with long-range rods, heavy line and boilies – in fact thousands of them! This was in complete contrast to Mike's methods whose delicate, light approach was directed to the margins! It was, however, the boiled bait approach coupled with long-range fishing that was to dominate the fishing during that season, and many carp came to the bank as a consequence.

Many of these anglers in that first syndicate are still heavily involved in the carp scene today, and some of the biggest fish they had ever caught came in that first year at Savay. Some of the best stories have never been told; others by contrast have been flogged to death. In 1980, with hindsight, carp fishing was a brave new world, and developments in presentation and effective baits were pushed to the fore. Andy Little and a few others used the revolutionary hair rig, which in conjunction with a hard boiled bait proved more than a match for the Savay carp. It was an onslaught from which the Savay carp took some time to recover.

In all fairness, however, it was still the best anglers that caught the most fish. Rod Hutchinson had a bumper year, with his uncanny knack of finding feeding fish time after time. Carp weighing 30lb were being caught in a greater quantity than ever before. Many captures stand out during this year, one being the magnificent 30lb mirror that John Baker caught.

This capture was watched by many of the syndicate as they gathered around John one afternoon as he played this most powerful fish that refused to come anywhere near the bank. Con-

stant pressure by John eventually brought a very big carp within netting range. It was a prized 'Leney' mirror and one that provided John Baker with the highlight of his angling career at the time.

Lenny Middleton was another special carp angler who holds a place in carp fishing history. Besides being the inventor of the hair rig he put a good number of Savay carp on the bank that year. The largest, however, was foulhooked (and he admitted it), all 34lb 4oz of it. But this special year belonged to Rod Hutchinson and Andy Little. Who says the good guys don't always win?

These two were head and shoulders above the rest – admittedly they fished very hard and spent a great amount of time at the fishery, but others did too. It was location, the age-old ingredient, that Rod and Andy had off to a fine art. Good bait and the hair rig helped, of course, but putting the bait in an area where the carp were feeding or were going to feed was the key to success. Andy Little alone put forty-three carp of over 20lb on the bank between June and November, and Rod wasn't far behind either. The incredible multiple catches occurred when huge shoals of quality carp descended on the heavily baited areas that Rod and Andy had prepared. Three, four or more big carp came to the net when everything gelled together.

Savay was in the open and the full ramification of its place in history was sealed.

## OTHER CARP

I have made little mention of the actual fish themselves during the last few pages of this Savay chronicle. So, let us look at what had happened by the time the 1980 season ended. The original two batches of Leney carp would be in their thirtieth year by then. However, the largest carp to come from the fishery – a little over 34lb – was a long orange-coloured, fast-fighting 'Dutch' fish. This carp, and indeed several others over 30lb captured in the 1980 season, came mostly from a stocking of 100 14in fish in 1966. These were purchased from Stambridge Trout Fisheries near Rochford in Essex. The stocking took place in early December 1966, but it appears that there were few mortalities for many of these fish weighed at least 25lb in weight.

Another famous stocking of carp, and yet another different strain, was made in 1963. This consignment came from a small trout farm at Cirencester in Gloucestershire. The Bibury Trout Farm received an order from the Ruislip club during July, the 200 fish being delivered in the autumn of the same year. These were of an 'Italian' stock. Again, they grew well in Savay's fertile waters. Characterized by the very 'gutty' appearance – big stomachs and high backs – they became a feature of the catches that Mike Wilson had made in the 1970s as well as providing 'personal bests' for some of the syndicate members in 1980.

In all, from 1950 to 1974 Savay was to receive a grand total of some 2,500 carp, and of these nearly 1,000 were from the Surrey Trout Farm. Mike Wilson wrote the following in 1980:

'Assuming a growing period of 15 years from birth, and a growth rate, of say, 2.8lb per year for 14 years, plus, say, 8oz for the first year, then fish approaching 40lb could be found. This assumption is, however 0.8lb per year higher than known growth rates.

'In the first 16 years (1950–1966), 900 fish were stocked by Mr Leney, 200 Italian fish from Bibury and 100 from Stambridge. Leney's first 500 odd fish would have been 8–9 years old when the first of these fish were added.

'Without mortalities, there would be some 1230 fish at their peak by 1980. However, if we assumed a 90 per cent survival rate of the first 500 (a loss of 50 fish), and a 50 per cent survival rate of the 1962 and 1965 stocking of 300 fish (Leney), we would arrive at 690 fish. I have discounted the Bibury and Stambridge stocks due to their unknown source. If only 0.5 per cent represents the stock at maximum growth, then this would result in 3 of 4 fish around the 40lb mark. 2 to 3 per cent made this at Redmire (in the early 50s), the fish having more or less been left undis-

turbed, with little angling pressure. All stocking will have peaked by 1985.

'The next five years, assuming we can still fish the water under existing rules, must produce the finest chance for a very big fish.

'Of catfish, 5 are believed to have been introduced from Bedfordshire in 1971, with a further 6 in with a tench stocking by Anglo Aquarium. Not withstanding this, I am certain that there are others, as I hooked a fish in 1977 which was definitely not a carp or pike and I played it for over an hour until I ran out of line (10lb) and broke. Clive Diedrich also foulhooked a fish in 1979 or 1980 which he played for a long time and brought back a piece of mottled skin! It has been my long held view that there are damn great cats in Savay, which we know nothing about.'

Mike has not changed this view much over the last dozen years. However, although the water record for a carp is now over 45lb in weight (a Dutch fish, I think, and heavy with spawn), no catfish have, as far as I know, been landed.

## BIG, BIG CARP

There are now many fish in Savay that hold a special place in carp fishing history – none more so than Sally the common carp. Mike Wilson's immaculate records and pictures have enabled us to follow Sally throughout her life from when she was first captured in the early 1970s. Aside from the disfigurement of scales on the right-hand flank, it is perhaps the nick out of the top of her tail that is the real give-away – besides her huge size, that is! She damaged her tail originally when Mike Wilson caught her in the mid-1970s, and it never grew back although it did heal up. This carp grew and grew, at one stage putting on 4½lb in just four months.

These days this common carp is one of the enigmas of Savay, having gained an almost mythological status. It is now some years since she has been to the bank, and if you believe the stories that circulate through the fishery then she swam out of the lake a while ago when the bank

*The Leney legend lives on. Bob Copeland with a cracking 33lb Savay mirror landed from the Cottage Bay during the autumn of 1992.*

flooded at the southern end by the sluices. However, there have been many reports of her sighting by people I trust, some of which have been quite recent. These sightings could, of course, have been of another giant common carp, but the impression I get is that they were of Sally. What weight is she, I hear you ask. Well this could be a record fish!

There are other monsters in Savay, as ones have been seen from time to time. As long ago as 1978 very big fish indeed were spotted – take this instance from Mike Wilson's diary:

'One fish was under the trees by the canal gate and, as usual, Clive Diedrich and I were in the trees, only feet away. Having identified marks on a branch in line with head and tail, I was later able to notch a twig and measure it at home. It measured 43½in. I never saw that fish again.'

Since the author has fished the water during the last couple of years, I too have heard stories that make the hair on the back of your neck prickle! So far none of these monsters has been landed, although the lake has produced three great carp over 40lb in weight, the most recent being a magnificent 40lb 15oz mirror – though this was not a Leney fish.

I will now bring you bang up to date, with a report of the recent capture of one of the old Leney warriors. This carp figures way back in Mike Wilson's captures several times, but it was when the syndicate started in the early 1980s that it was a big fish. Rod Hutchinson caught this carp late one year after a night of enthusiastic celebration. In the morning he was feeling far from well. This glorious mirror weighed over 30lb in weight and provided a welcome relief for Rod's headache! Later Rod understandably nicknamed the carp 'Thick head', and that name has stuck ever since.

Anyway, this oft-caught biggie has figured in Savay catches ever since, and only recently appeared on the bank after picking up a bait that Bob Copeland had carefully cast out into the Cottage Bay. At well over 30lb it is, I think, the largest carp Bob has caught from Savay. One thing, however, is for sure – it was surely older than him!

# 7 THE ARMY LAKE – A LATE STARTER

*Never can this 'Leney' water be described as the most romantic carp lake in the land, but it did provide many exciting moments for me, with some of the finest-looking big carp it is possible to imagine!*

## BACKGROUND AND HISTORY

There is a large lake close to where I live, and which is situated just on the Surrey–Hampshire border. Surprisingly, it has commanded little in the way of attention from carp anglers over the years. However, the main interest and appeal of this lake lies within two sources, each of which has little to do with angling. The first is the British Army, and the second is television! I'd better explain.

The land surrounding this area belongs to the Ministry of Defence, as does most in the general vicinity. The 8th Royal Engineers live here and, as can be imagined with many troubles afoot, security is high. With this in mind, it's a wonder to me that we have not lost our access to this water, but as the battalion has a strong fishing club, voices other than ours make sure we still can fish – for the time being anyway.

The BBC also use this whole area as a back-cloth to stage the occasional programme called

*The open expanse of the Army Lake.*

'Run the Gauntlet' – usually on television around Christmas. The lake's setting is perfect for this with its large open area of water and several interesting islands. The programme sees contestants running around doing all manner of action things, including water sports, and using amphibious vehicles. Being on Royal Engineers' property, so to speak, the 'props' are already to hand! There is a huge sprawling concrete area within the Royal Engineers' compound that allows easy access for the amphibious crafts into the water, and this feature alone gives the lake little appeal as somewhere from which to catch a large carp!

The land here is similar to other areas around these parts, having sandy ground and being heavily wooded in this case with vast areas of pine trees. The general topography has little in the way of hills or any higher ground, so one gets the feeling of being out in the wide open air, if that's the way to describe it. Certainly, as you stand in one of the swims on the north bank and look out over the water, the far bank seems a long way off, although the water's 60-odd acres is broken up into manageable chunks by the islands. The latter have been doctored in more recent years by the local sailing club, no doubt to give a clear view so that they can check whether one of their fraternity has tipped up or gone missing out on the water.

This water has been in existence for many years, although originally it was man-made and still bears the mark of man's hand to this day. The most striking part of the lake's appearance is the wonderful rhododendron bushes that cover the greater part of the perimeter. In the early summer they make for a colourful setting and add greatly to the lake's appeal – that is, if you don't look towards the Army area. The water is not deep for most of the expanse – perhaps 8ft in a number of places – generally you'll find it to be between 3 and 5ft. Shallow water means weed, and lots of it. I'm not sure what species it is, but

*Besides the Army, anglers had the problem of the boating members.*

it's tough and very wiry. This, coupled with the fact that for most of the time the water is cloudy, makes spotting fish difficult. But the carp do show themselves either by leaping or by some kind of disturbance on the surface.

The stocks of fish present can be divided into two types. First, there are the usual sort of fish: tench, bream, roach, rudd, perch and pike. The second, consist of guess what? That's right, carp. These were stocked into the lake in 1956, and the Surrey Trout Farm delivery note shows 200 4–5in king carp were introduced (the size denotes that they were one-year olds). As with other waters discussed within this book, the 1950s saw a massive rise in the introduction of king carp to British waters. Also in common with most waters, the carp at Army Lake were never fished for during their formative and, more importantly, growing years. In fact, carp anglers never came on the scene at the Army Lake until the late 1960s.

Naturally enough, some carp were landed and recently I met a gentleman who claimed to have landed an 18lb mirror in 1963 – the year after the big freeze-up. Sadly, he has not managed to find a photograph, but his description of a mirror carp with scales all along the middle of the long body sounds right. He also saw another carp caught during the summer of 1964 that weighed 'just over 20lb'. A turning point in the lake's development came later in the decade. A few local specimen hunters turned their attention to the Army Lake. Stories of big carp had been circulating for some time, and anglers such as these always kept their ears open to the possibility of new venues.

Although most stories concerning big carp were often of a dubious nature, they had in this case stumbled upon a rich wealth of carp fishing – many of the carp were in the 20lb class and were not wise in the ways of anglers.

Of the many baits in use at the time, it was floating crust that was to be the eventual undoing of these carp. Because of the nature of the banks, it meant that most areas had 3ft of water directly in the margins and this made them ideal for floating crust methods. When all was quiet at night, and with the anglers quietly secreting

themselves away (no night fishing was allowed), they caught many of these carp by fishing a crust directly under the rod tip within a few feet of the bank. Maximum stealth was required, and quiet at all times was essential. The introduction of loose crusts once darkness had descended often had the carp investigating. This method was developed by Richard Walker just prior to World War II and was to have a major impact on the realization by many that uncatchable carp could become catchable!

The excitement of fishing in this style, especially at night, makes it addictive – it must have been all the more so when one thinks of the size of the fish present in the lake at the time, the bulk being between 18lb and 22lb. Because of the high numbers of carp caught, a decision was taken to move some fish to other waters in the area. Although we frown upon this kind of action these days, and quite rightly, twenty years ago the anglers concerned really thought they were doing both the fish and the waters concerned a favour. Indeed, one of the lakes on the receiving end of a batch of these carp became a famous water in its own right, and in the late 1970s produced several fish over 30lb with one approaching 40lb! Another lake that gained these introductions also became a terrific carp water, and was one that offered free fishing! I can reveal as I write now that some of these relocated carp are still being caught at this water and that the fishing is still free.

How many fish were removed from the Army Lake is unclear, but it was considerable and, along with fatalities that happen as a matter of course during such an action, meant that come the 1980s few of the original 200 carp were still swimming around. Although it is always difficult to estimate the population of carp in large lakes such as this, captures seem to suggest that less than thirty big carp live here now. Work this out and you'll find that each of these carp has 2 acres to itself! Matters are made worse by the fact that the boating people are out in all the daylight hours and a motorboat roars about the place making sure that all know the budding Walter Raleighs are about! Oh, I forgot, there are water-

*Jan Wenczka with an early, long, lean 'tiger nut' caught fish – 23lb.*

skiers there as well. Now, if all this sounds almost too much for you to contemplate, the final blow comes from the Army. What with night manoeuvres, amphibious crafts, divers and squads of Army men always running about the place, it really can be terrible. However, I think that this just has to be endured, because there are some cracking carp in here – the wonderful 'Leney' strain of long, lean fighting machines with beautiful scaling and averaging around the 25lb mark.

It has now been some years since several carp fishing friends and I became interested in this most demanding water. It was the time of the 'tiger nut' phenomenon (1984), and we decided that this would be the way to attack the water. We found that an area into which the carp came frequently was a fairly large bay. This was also comparatively sheltered from the activities of the non-angling public, although fishing this area after 10 a.m. was hit and miss. I found that the period from first light to 9.30 a.m. offered the best chance of a run. Our little band of anglers managed to land several of these prized carp as the fish became used to finding bait in our heavily baited areas. However, it was tough going, with a fish only coming every now and then. It was during one of these early-morning sessions that a breakthrough came for me that was to have far-reaching effects in the years to come.

## FLOATING BAIT BREAKTHROUGH

The morning had become hot again as I sat half-hidden in the rhododendrons. Little had happened, although far out in the lake over to the right a big fish had jumped at first light. Even though that carp had jumped some 150yd away, the ripples came over to me and broke the mirror-like surface. I wondered what fish it might be, and how big it was. Was it going to come anywhere near my bed of bait? All, however, was quiet, and I fell asleep as the sun came up and the day burst forth in all its glory. It was the muffled noise some time later of a boat being launched that made me stir and shake my head. Good grief, it was nearly 9 a.m. – I'd nodded off for nearly eighty minutes! A breeze had sprung up and the lake looked so different now, more hostile than in the hushed dawn of a few hours before. As I looked out into the distance, I could see the vague forms of Army personnel alighting on to the water. Time was running out, and it was time to call it a day – at least on this water anyway. Thoughts were already drifting to another lake and to a day off I had from work – it's a great life if you can get it!

Hanging on until the very last minute of my fishing time is something I've done now for years, for often a chance has come in these last moments. I stood by my rods – which were just supported by the front rod rests only – while everyone else packed away. I carefully scanned the water just in case any movement was evident. Of course, just as I was fiddling about in my tackle bag and not looking at the water, suddenly a heavy splash occurred over to the right, tight to the rhododendrons. This was well into the bay, and in a place in which I have never seen big fish move. 'That's interesting', I thought and as I looked...*Crash!* He did it again. It looked a good fish as it almost stood on its tail before entering the water in what seemed like slow motion.

These moments with carp are one of the great attractions of the fish, and can make the hair on your neck bristle and your mouth go dry. With this occurrence happening I quickly reeled in my rods, checking that the baits had not been interfered with! I decided that after I'd been back to the car and packed everything away I would have a look at the spot where the big carp had jumped. Could I get anywhere near to the water at that point? I'd investigate...

Besides some tiger nuts, I picked up a bag of Chum Mixer, just in case. Until this point I had not actively thought of surface baits for once as a means to catch one of these fish. Saying that, I always have thoughts of these baits on my mind. When I looked at this particular part of the lake I noticed that a small path led into the rhododendrons at this point. Where did it lead to? I had to find out.

However, to my dismay after only 10yd or so it seemed to finish – but wait, looking further I could see a tunnel through the rhododendrons. Perhaps this was used by the Army while on combat trials, or perhaps it was only mischievous boys making a camp here in the summer holidays? I made my mind up to investigate further.

Once inside this tunnel the available light was cut by half and the floor of the path was covered by a layer of dead leaves – not the sort that crunch noisily under foot but the kind that allows you silent passage. The water was only a few feet away to my left. It seemed to be almost illuminated, this effect being produced by the fact that no light was coming in from the overhanging rhododendrons, but bright light from the outside penetrated to give this weird effect.

There was just enough room to allow access along this route as I made my way. After 20yd I stopped, thinking it must be close to where that fish had jumped. At this point I pushed through the tough rhododendron branches and peered into the water.

There was no mistaking the shape of five big carp lying just a few feet from my eyes! I froze, caught my breath and slowly crouched. The nearest fish to the bank was so close to the surface that his back was out of the water, and he looked unconcerned as we watched one another almost eyeball to eyeball! This was a tremendous looking fish, was very long – at least 30in – and displayed that 'Leney' speciality (it was a linear carp), having mirror scales of the same size perfectly along the lateral line. He was just opening and closing his mouth and looked like he would be a prime candidate for a piece of Chum Mix.

But enough of him; the other four carp present were beauties too. Every one looked over 20lb, and on first inspection none of them looked any larger than another. After this, several of the fish slowly moved around the general area and it was clear then that one in particular was much bigger. In practice, when you look at fish in the water if one looks a bit bigger you can bet that when you land it it will be a good deal heavier. I thought this carp could have been approaching 30lb. All the big carp present were mirrors and were in super condition. One came in close to the bank almost under my feet, but it was different – paler than the rest and displaying a high back and greater depth. It must have weighed around the 25lb mark.

I moved back and reached down into the bag of Chum Mixer. What should I do? I decided to throw some in over to the right as there was a ripple coming in from right to left anyway. With the Chum scattered over the area, several pieces soon came in on the drift, just as I had hoped. In any moment they would come into vision of the linear fish and the pale coloured mirror. One piece of Chum in particular arrived right over the mouth of the linear – what would it do? Well it never moved, and didn't even cock its eye upwards. Another couple of bits came close to the other carp, but again there was no reaction.

I threw some more out and wondered what would happen this time. Suddenly, there was a swirl. The first batch of Chum had become lodged against some branches and the linear was at it. Then the other mirror was by his side and up it came as well, another piece gone. 'That's it!' I thought. 'Where's my rod?'

*The pale one – the author's first big fish to Chum Mixer.*

This was easier said than done, however, for I tried to extract myself from the clinging branches, never giving myself enough time, and caught my T-shirt and ripped it. But soon I was back in the tunnel and was travelling back towards the open area. Once there I started to half-run/half-walk back to the car. After a hasty tackle up and having checked that everything was in order, it was back into the tunnel. I must explain that both my rod and landing net were broken down – this was a great aid as I tried to squeeze myself, plus the tackle, along this tight passageway. Once back at the place where the fish were, I quickly checked they were still in evidence...although their positions had changed, all the five carp were still there.

Up went my rod (the bait was already in position) and after much struggling I got the landing net in the right place. As I have already explained, this area was tight, but not that tight. I figured a hooked fish would shoot out under the canopy into clearer, deeper water. If I was strong and firm I felt that I could man-handle the fish back under the canopy and into the waiting net.

Getting into position I was pleased to find that my antics had not aroused the carp, so all was well. There was no Chum left, so very carefully I flicked out half a dozen more pieces using just my thumb. These again came down in the ripple, but as they approached three of the carp I now had my hookbait just dangling off the rod tip. This was it, the half-chance I needed. The linear spotted the Chum, moved slightly forward, and a piece disappeared. Shakily, I dropped the hookbait next to this fish. He ignored it at first, but turned just as another carp accelerated from the left. They both shot forward together, and it seemed that they were on a collision course with my hook-bait in the middle of it all!

A fraction of a second later an almighty wrench came on the rod top. What happened in those first few seconds remains a blur but immediately I thrust the rod tip under the water. The ancient Mitchell reel begrudgingly gave line just at the last moment and saved the day. The fish twisted and turned on a short line right on the edge of the canopy. He hung there out of reach, and time almost stood still, my mind racing at what to do next. The net (one with small throat to it) was half man-handled into place. In one hair-raising moment the fish slid sideways over the net...that was it!

For a few seconds or so I couldn't move, my heart was pumping like fury and my head started to swim. But as everything came back into focus I managed to drag the net and fish up on to the bank. It was a big fish. The depth was really impressive and had me guessing straight away that perhaps here was a 25lb carp. To cut a long

*Steve Sorrel (with head missing) shows off the most spectacular-looking Army Lake carp. It personifies all that is special about a Galician carp.*

story short, I managed to get myself, the fish, and net back into an open area. Once there, it was accurately weighed and turned the scales at 23lb 8oz. Upon inspection it proved to be the paler carp, and it was lightly scaled but totally unmarked with a great big mouth. Now I had the yardstick – I knew there and then that the slightly larger looking fish must have been 5lb heavier!

*A double-row linear carp, the likes of which you just don't see any more.*

## A 'LENEY' TO REMEMBER!

This 'chink in the armour' in the behaviour of the Army Lake's carp – Chum fished under the rhododendrons – has proved to be a winner for me. The years have rolled by with several other big carp falling to the same method, and culminating in the finest, most staggeringly good looking big carp I have ever seen. The account of its capture, which occurred within the last few days (or should I say hours) of the 1989/90 season, gladdens my heart so that it has become the angling highlight of my career...so far!

For me, I achieved a carp angling feat I thought might be difficult in the extreme – even in this day and age. That is, a really big carp

*Young angler Brian Hook, who fished long and hard at the Army Lake, caught a number of carp. This sparsely scaled beauty came in the school holidays!*

caught off the surface in the winter. Successful fishing on the top in winter is something I've enjoyed in the past, so I was aware of exactly what was possible. However, the waters where I tried this approach were in the main places where there were no carp that topped that magical 30lb mark. When I landed a twenty-pounder some years ago, I knew it was one of only a few of that weight that had been deliberately caught in this fashion in the winter.

In the back of my mind I considered my recent affair with the mighty Savay in the Colne Valley and thought that this might be the place to try (and it might still be), but in truth the time and effort involved was a commitment I couldn't afford in terms of work. Time had been tight for fishing since the start of 1990, so somewhere close was the order of the day. But where? Places that hold 30lb carp in my neck of the woods are often crowded throughout the year these days. In the end I decided that there really was nowhere to go unless I had the time to look at Savay...

So, winter carp fishing for me during that time was restricted to an odd few sessions at that excellent day-ticket water near Aldershot: Willow Park. The bobbins really flew and several very nice looking carp were landed, sometimes in very cold conditions and in darkness too (it was unusual for me to be out after dark at my age!).

Suddenly it was near the season's end. I telephoned my long-time friend Jan and suggested we meet up with Andy Little at Willow for the last day together. It would be a light-hearted affair – we had not had the opportunity to fish together for ages – and there was also every chance of a run or two. Jan had never before been to Willow, so with conditions remaining settled for the next few days, chances were looking rather promising. On the Tuesday morning (10 March) I telephoned the owner of Raison Bros, John Raison, to check if it was OK for Jan to come.

'He can come, but he can't fish, there's a match on!' reported John.

'Oh, that's a shame,' I said, 'What time does it finish?'

'5 p.m.' said John.

That ruled it out. I contacted Andy and said,

*In amongst the Leney fish you would often get the linear type. This Army Lake carp came to Chum Mixer fished under the rhododendrons.*

'Why don't we try Broadwater Lake?'

Andy was less than keen, however, for he was off to France on the last day of the season and was due to leave for the ferry around 4 p.m. He said, 'If I can't fish locally, I'll knock it on the head.'

Although I was unaware of it at the time, fate was starting to deal me a good hand and was paving the way to a big fish...

I contacted Jan on the Tuesday morning to say that the plans were scuppered – mind you, he came straight back with the suggestion that I join him at one of his waters. But somehow I didn't

fancy that either. I was restless and said, 'If we can't all fish together as originally planned, I go my own way.'

The forecast looked good for Wednesday and Thursday, and when I returned home from work on the Tuesday evening the air was warm and still – just right, in fact. That evening as I sat in the Carproom with the sunset slanting strongly through the windows and clutching a glass of port, my mind began to wander...

I wondered if those carp at the Army Lake would be stirring under the rhododendrons. After all, rhododendrons don't lose their leaves,

*Mild conditions prevailed during the last few days of the season.*

so the heat loss would be marginal. Maybe, just maybe, the carp might be there, back in their old haunts.

Racing away from London, the car went faster and faster as we sped westwards along the M3 at breakneck speed. It was nearly 3 p.m. when I finally pulled up in the car-park. The weather was glorious - what a beautiful day it was – all the tackle was ready and so was the Chum!

Along the path I scuttled, and with the sun streaming down it felt unbelievably hot. Would those carp be there? The excitement was rising. Right, let's see. I darted into the undergrowth and along a rhododendron tunnel. The last time I had been here was the previous September, and strangely enough, because the bushes do not lose their leaves, it all looked the same and bore no signs of the winter that had passed.

I stopped at the first available spot and looked through the branches – nothing. So, continuing just a few paces more, I looked again. Well, well, what's this I see? Is it a carp? I blinked…of course it was, and another, and yet another. These were comparatively small fish and were swimming quite close to the surface.

Out went the Chum – several handfuls of it – and soon to my delight a fish showed interest, taking several pieces. This was fine, but were there any of the big old 'Leney' fish about? Within fifteen minutes I found out the answer to this, for there swimming past, only feet from where I lay hidden, was one of these fantastic fish. It displayed a deep blue-purple back and had a tail which was like the span of two hands.

It came past again a few moments later, and as it swam away it came up and took a piece of surface food as though it hadn't a care in the world. Some Chum had drifted along in the light ripple away to the left, where I couldn't get a hookbait, of course.

*A rhododendron tunnel – the way to a big fish.*

It was looking as if catching one of these fish was possible. That feeling that only carp can generate started to surge around my body. This was it – the very essence of why I go carp fishing, the closeness of the fish, big fish, and the chance of catching one.

The trap was laid and it was only a matter of time before the big fish would reappear. The tackle and net were in position, with the hookbait already hanging off the rod tip and hovering just above the water. Other smaller carp joined in the feeding spree, any one of which I could have hooked easily, but they were half the size of the blue-backed mirror.

The tension mounted, and my eyes darted left and right straining to see the big fish should it approach – then there it was. It took a piece of Chum only a couple of feet away before entering the critical zone, the area where I stood a chance of hooking and landing it. The hookbait kissed the water's surface, up came the fish, down the hatch went the bait, and 'whack'…after two quick lunges, the rod sprang back and nearly threw me off balance. What had happened? The fish was gone. I swore…badly. The hookhold had given, but when I looked everything was OK – it was just 'sod's law' I'm afraid. I sat there shaking – how could I have got it so right, yet everything went so wrong? I went back to the car for a breather.

Ten minutes later I returned. I wondered if there would be any carp left in the swim. My luck was in, for a couple were about. I thought I would try again, and after 20 minutes or so these two carp were showing interest. Both were in the 10–15lb range and not what I was really after. I watched them as they showed no caution when taking the bait, then close to the bank and almost unnoticed by me sneaked a good fish which turned and came into the swim.

I lowered the hookbait, and as with the first fish this carp came up without hesitation and took it. This time good fortune was with me, and after a lot of crashing about, into the folds of the net it went. Great stuff, for I had really thought I wouldn't get another chance. It was a nice fish, but not as big as I first thought. On the scales it was spot on at 18lb. 'That'll do,' I thought.

It was time to go home, but I'd be back the next day for sure.

This day was the last day of the 1989/90 season, and one I take off work on most years. But what a different day it turned out to be, weather-wise. It was so cold compared to the previous one. I did some work at home before setting out on that last foray of the season. As the day progressed it got even colder! By 2.30 p.m. I was back in position, inside the tunnel of rhododendrons. No fish at first were present, but after a while I saw just two, which by contrast to the previous day were swimming much deeper. None came up for any bait and the situation looked grim. I sat waiting for over an hour, but besides the odd small carp, nothing looked remotely as if it would come up to investigate the surface bait.

'That's it,' I decided, 'I'll go and try another water for the last few hours of daylight.' On the way back to the car I hesitated at a spot where the rhododendrons and the lake came to an end. It was at just this point that I'd managed to catch one or two carp the previous summer. 'I'll just check,' I thought.

It turned out to be the best thing I ever did that season!

That momentary pause, followed by my stopping to look in this swim shows just how fate or luck can change events drastically.

When I pushed through the branches and looked in the water there were three big dark shapes. By then it was gone 3.30 p.m. and the daylight was beginning to drain away under heavy cloud cover, for it was quite dark under the rhododendrons.

Almost as soon as it was out, the loose Chum was inspected by a nice fish of 15–20lb. It came back for more. I'd seen enough, and removing myself carefully from the undergrowth I reached for the rod, bag and net. It was very tight inside this rhododendron bush but somehow I managed to get everything organized without arousing the carp's suspicion. All was set! Some more Chum was thrown out and the three carp circled close by just a few inches below the surface. Now, would they come back into the area where it was safe to present a hookbait? I watched as the Chum drifted away to the left, when suddenly a huge orange mouth engulfed a piece. Good God, what was that? Again the fish came up and took another piece – what a huge mouth! In a flash I decided that orifice must belong to a whopper! Then a disaster nearly happened. I just caught sight of a fish coming up under the hookbait, and I quickly withdrew it – it was the hungry one, the fish I'd spotted first.

By then I was seriously starting to get the collywobbles, for here was an outstanding chance. I lowered the Chum once again on to the surface just under the rod tip, but it was dithering in the water, my hands were shaking so! I draped it over a tiny twig – that helped and at least it kept still.

Within thirty seconds I had to take it off the surface again as the same hungry fish came back and looked at the bait very hard. This fish was stationary, almost directly under the bait even though it was 2in off the surface! It didn't move, and only then did I realize that it might try to reach out of the surface and have a go at the bait. I quickly drew it higher – just in case!

I was waiting for the big fish with the huge orange mouth to come out in the open. Eventually it did so and the Chum was lowered right in its path. Up it came, seemingly in slow motion...

The Chum disappeared down the hatch and a quick flick of the rod tip produced a violent wrench on the rod. I held on – like fury! The big carp thrashed the water to a froth, but I never let him get his head down. Bundling the net into the water and with the carp held on a tight line, within thirty seconds I somehow – though how I actually did this is lost in the excitement – man-handled the fish into it. 'What a relief!' I shouted out.

With my heart pounding almost out of my chest I slumped in a heap amongst the rhododendron branches. It took perhaps a minute for me to come round again. When I did so, I drew the net upwards, tight around the fish. Looking inside it was dark, but there was my prize. I felt the weight, or should I say I tried to – it was too heavy to lift! With the net wedged between the branches I bit the line, and with two hands I manhandled the whole lot up and over the branches on to dry land.

The carp was in a tight U-shape inside the net – I remember clearly as I gently put the heavy load on to the soft ground that the carp uncurled! There in the net lay a tremendous fish...it was a monster!

As I sorted out the weighsling and keepsack, my eyes never left the fish. I thought that it must be close to, if not over 30lb. My mind was spinning. Soon, up on the scales it went. Yes, I'd done it!

A short time later Duncan, my eldest son, and one of the twins Martyn, arrived along with a capable cameraman and we checked the weight again.

Out in the open this carp was a staggering sight to witness in all its winter glory – red and gold all over, with linear scaling, some scales being 3–4in long. Wow!

At 31lb 8oz it might be the largest ever winter floater-caught carp!

This carp was possibly the finest looking 'Leney' I've ever landed. From its nose to the tip of its tail it measured an unbelievable 36¼in. It was a magical fish that had grown from a tiny 5in baby when stocked in 1956 to become some thirty-five years later one of the high spots of my angling career.

*The kind of carp you just dream about...Leney magic!*

# INDEX